Earned Wisdom

Becoming an Elder in Times of Chaos

Julie Simmons

Order this book online at www.trafford.com
or email orders@trafford.com

Most Trafford titles are also available at major online book retailers.

Printed in the United States of America.

ISBN: 978-1-4269-9494-4 (sc)
ISBN: 978-1-4269-9495-1 (e)

Trafford rev. 11/15/2011

Trafford PUBLISHING www.trafford.com

North America & international
toll-free: 1 888 232 4444 (USA & Canada)
phone: 250 383 6864 • fax: 812 355 4082

This book is dedicated to those who "continue to grow old, instead of merely sinking into the aging process."—Helen M. Luke, from *Old Age*

And to my mother, Eva, who had a terrible time differentiating between a blessing and a curse.

"I believe in old age; to work and to grow old: this is what life expects of us. And then one day to be old and still quite far from understanding everything—no, but to begin, but to love, but to suspect, but to be connected to what is remote and inexpressible, all the way up to the stars."

—Rainer Maria Rilke,
The Poet's Guide to Life: The Wisdom of Rilke

CONTENTS

Introduction

Age is opportunity no less,
Than youth itself, though in another dress.
And as the evening twilight fades away,
The sky is filled with stars invisible by day.
—H.W. Longfellow, *Morituri Salutamus*

In the twenty-first century, more and more of us are living for decades past sixty. We are redefining "old age," finding ways to remain active in our communities and seeking a new role for ourselves. This transition—becoming an elder—can be just as daunting as every other major life transition (childhood to adolescence, adolescence to young adult, young adult to mature adult, and now, mature adult to elder). We need to use all the navigational tools we can gather, and seek out those who have successfully made the transition before us.

For thirty-five years I have been a counselor, teacher and writer on astrology. It has informed my way of seeing the world, and its gifts have been many and varied. The sole drawback to being an astrologer has been that many people don't know enough about this discipline. There is a general lack of understanding about the practical ways in which astrology can help to navigate life, especially during times of change, whether internal (such as a life transition) or external (such as a chaotic political and economic climate). In my own sixtieth year, I have written this book to serve as a guide for those on the journey to becoming an elder, and those looking back and trying to better understand the changes they have lived through.

Astrology offers wisdom and insight into the human condition, developed over thousands of years. It is a language of symbols as ancient as the first person who ever noticed a connection between the waxing and waning Moon and the behavior of humans, plants and animals. In his thought-provoking book on human evolution, *Sex, Time and Power,* Leonard Shlain speaks of what it must have been like to be among the first people to make the connection between the cycle of the Moon and the cycle of women. This may have been the first symbolic thought.[1] Certainly it was the first major astrological thought. The ability to relate that which is above to that which is below allows us to understand ourselves as part of the universe instead of apart from it. The ability to see ourselves reflected in nature encourages us to feel the connection between our inner reality and the outer one. As we say in astrology: "As above, so below."

From these ancient beginnings, astrology has evolved into a language of archetypes. As Richard Tarnas wrote in *Cosmos and Psyche*, archetypes can be seen as "autonomous patterns of meaning that inform both psyche and matter, providing a bridge between inner and outer."[2] In my imagination, at the dawn of creation—the Big Bang, as we now understand it—patterns or archetypes as well as material forms manifested with the explosion. These patterns inform existence. They are invisible to the human eye because they are pure energy. They seem to permeate everything. Each and every person as well as everything in nature is a manifestation of these archetypal patterns. It is said that you cannot look upon the face of God and live. If you think of God as the ultimate archetype, the One that encompasses the All, the whole that is greater than the sum of its parts, it makes sense that it would be impossible to see God through the lens of the physical body the very essence of which is to experience yourself as separate. What we, the living, the manifest, see is that which is manifest. The way we approach the archetypal world is through myth. Max Müller, the nineteenth-century German scholar who created the discipline of comparative religion, wrote:

> Mythology is inevitable, it is natural, it is an inherent necessity of language, if we recognize in language the outward form and manifestation of thought; it is in fact the dark shadow which language throws upon thought, and which can never disappear . . . Depend upon it, there is mythology now as there was in the time of Homer, only we do not perceive it.[3]

The most effective way to approach archetypal patterns is through myth and metaphor. Joseph Campbell, the great twentieth-century scholar of myth and religion, once said: "It would not be too much to say that myth is the secret opening through which the inexhaustible energies of the cosmos pour into human cultural manifestation."[4] The "inexhaustible energies of the cosmos" are the archetypal patterns that inform the manifest world. Myth is the metaphor through which we can understand how archetypal principles work at any given time in history. Astrology speaks to us through myth and metaphor and enables us to understand the nature of things that work under the radar of our rational minds.

As a practicing astrologer for more than three decades, I have found the symbolic language of astrology to be an incredible help in navigating my own life as well as the lives of my clients. In particular, I have found in the discipline of astrology an exceptional language for framing all manner of transitions. In school we were taught the difference between a sign and a symbol: a sign is something you look *at,* a symbol is something you look *through.* Oddly enough, the twelve primary symbolic constructs of astrology are called signs (Aries, Taurus, Gemini, Cancer, Leo, Virgo, Libra, Scorpio, Sagittarius, Capricorn, Aquarius, and Pisces). Nonetheless they function as symbols, and by looking through them we can see worlds upon worlds of meaning.

We live in times of chaos and change. Leaders come and go; the economy is in tatters. It has become more and more difficult to understand this chaotic world in the pure light of reason. We find ourselves in need of analogy and metaphor to help us see who we are in the swirling onslaught of too much information. Symbols and the underlying meaning they can reveal to us become more necessary in times of change.

Astrology is not a religion. It is a discipline and can serve as a navigational tool. Like language itself, it allows us to tell the story. The story it tells is a reflection of the experiences we have. It helps us to give context and meaning to our lives, according to the perspective of our culture and the times in which we live. James Hillman, a Jungian psychologist, has said:

> Mythological gods differ from those of religion . . . To paraphrase an ancient Roman defender of myth, Sallust: the gods of myth never happened but always are. Myths provide archetypal ways of insighting the human condition; they present psychological truths . . . Religion in contrast encodes a particular story as the revelation of a particular god's own word of immortal truth to a historical human in a specific place at a specific moment. Myths ask the psyche to invent and speculate, to listen and be amused; religion, first of all, calls for belief. [5]

Astrology partakes of the constantly changing nature of myth. Unlike religion, it changes to reflect the times in which the astrologer lives. We stand on the cusp of a new age: the end of one world (the Age of Pisces) and the beginning of a new one (the Age of Aquarius). Like all births it is a difficult and chaotic time with no guaranteed outcome. Astrology as a popular language reflects the culture, which is why it stays so relevant. In days of old Aries was the sign of the warrior, the soldier, the rebel. It still has that meaning, but today it is also associated with the modern athlete and, generally speaking, represents the urge to act as an individual, separate from the whole. Astrology speaks the language of the present even and especially when that present is chaotic and unpredictable.

Astrology holds the keys to the mythic reality of the times *even as it shifts.* The symbols of astrology allow us to navigate the river of our lives rather than control it. Many people have the mistaken belief that delving into astrology is a way to abdicate control over one's life. That is not how it works. Here is a simple analogy to convey how astrology works: The dance of the Sun, Moon, stars and planets in the heavens above is said to mirror our reality down below. It is a reflection. If you look in a mirror and you are having a bad hair day, you don't blame the mirror, you fix your hair. What we see reflected back at us from above allows us to see ourselves and the world in which we live. What we do with that information is up to us. Astrology is actually one of the most stunning and effective ways that we have for seeing and interpreting the transformation of our culture into the next age.

On September 11, 2001, when the twin towers of the World Trade Center in New York were attacked and destroyed, thousands died and one of the most powerful symbols of American capitalism was destroyed. People desperately tried to understand this event and how it would affect their lives. Astrology has offered some insightful perspectives. Pluto is the planet that symbolizes the powers of destruction and irrefutable change. On 9/11, it was in the sign of Sagittarius, which is associated with the notion of fundamental belief systems and the passion that people bring to defending their beliefs, their religion and their culture. Saturn, the planet of the status quo, the figure of authority and control over resources, was opposite Pluto in the sign of Gemini, symbolized by twins. An opposition means a challenge. Astrologically this opposition could be interpreted to suggest a picture of inevitable change, driven by fanatical conviction that the beliefs held by certain individuals or groups are *truth itself,* and thereby righteously justified in attacking the status quo as seen in the twin towers. The location of the Saturn Pluto opposition in the heavens on September 11, 2001 was almost exactly on the axis in the astrological chart of the United States that denotes challenge, conflict and war. [6]

It is possible to cast a horoscope for any event that has a place of birth as well as a date and time. The event that we are most familiar with in this regard is the birth or beginning of a human life. It is also possible to cast an astrological chart for a nation, a business, a marriage, or just about anything that you would like to understand through the lens of astrology.

Knowing these things doesn't take away the horror and the pain of loss, but it can help us to grapple with a world that will never be the same. One of astrology's most valuable gifts is that as it frames an event such as 9/11, it opens the door to discussion in a way that helps us to do more than simply theorize; it allows us to participate in the event itself. Knowing that Pluto was on the ascending sign of the United States at this terrible moment indicates that it was already in a condition of deep, destructive transformation. It suggests that a process of decline was already underway. The placement of Saturn on the opposite point, the point of "open enemies," indicated an enemy with a lot of staying power. In *Cosmos and Psyche,* Richard Tarnas describes periods when Saturn and Pluto interact as "historical periods marked by a pervasive quality of intense contraction: eras of international crisis and conflict, empowerment of reactionary forces and totalitarian impulses, organized violence and oppression, all sometimes marked by lasting traumatic effects." [7]

Astrology [8] gives us a way to catch a glimpse of how powerful archetypal patterns work within and around us. In a sense we are made of archetypal constructs or complexes. In our least aware moments we are often compelled to unconsciously act out these patterns. This is most distressing if the patterns are dysfunctional. If we grow up in difficult circumstances we must choose as adults to act out the past or awaken to the present. As we become more conscious of the energies that have shaped us, our awareness develops into a valuable tool that allows us to consider different possibilities in the ways we might use the energies that we embody.

This book grew out of a workshop that I teach for people over the age of fifty. I originally developed the workshop for two reasons. Through my years of counseling, I had noticed a specific astrological pattern starting around the age of fifty. Gradually it began to dawn on me that these astrological events plot a course through the transition from adult to elder. You start at fifty as a mature adult. You are actually in the last stages of adult life. By the time you are sixty, you have become a young elder. Making this transition with as much awareness as possible is extremely helpful in creating a context of meaning that allows us to take up residence in the elder period of our lives. It's a great help in navigating the transition from adult to elder as well as offering much insight in how to sustain the experience of being an elder after the age of sixty. It is never too late to do this work. No matter how long ago you might have turned fifty, the insights and understanding that come at the transition between adult and elder can guide and enrich the experience of being an elder even well into your eighties and beyond.

The second reason I developed the workshop was very personal. When I reached the age of fifty-five, I began to understand that the process of becoming an elder was not simply theoretical. It became clear that my life both inner and outer was changing. I realized that I was disoriented and confused as to how this period would be different than what I had been doing for most of my adult life. The strongest disorienting circumstance was that my only child was about to graduate high school and my role as mother was changing much faster than I was. I quite literally could not understand what was expected of me. That feeling combined with one of my most trusted axioms; if you really want to learn something, teach it. And so I was inspired to gather people together and see if, using what astrology suggests, I could ask the right questions and in so doing generate some insight into this stage of our lives.

I offer this book to you in the spirit of using it to ask the right questions. As we step into the rich, symbolic language of astrology to understand ourselves, we are engaging the unconscious. Some of what lives in our unconscious is personal—messages from our past that speak of forgotten or insufficiently understood experience. In another aspect of the unconscious—the collective unconscious—we discover things that resonate for all humans, across cultures. Using the universal symbols of astrology allows the dialogue between the known and the unknown to become stronger and enables us to catch profound glimpses of meaning that can enrich our experience.

Keeping a journal as you read through the material in this book will help create a very personal mirror for your experience of transition from adult to elder, whether you are in the midst of the process or have long since transitioned. For each topic I have created an exercise; you can find these exercises in Appendix II at the back of the book. The exercises are simply to help stimulate thoughts on any given subject. My hope is that by keeping a journal and possibly doing the exercises you will create a kind of personal manual for your own elderhood. Once you have completed this process you may find yourself, from time to time, lost in the experience of being an elder (rather than becoming one) you can refer to your journal and it will help orient you on the path. Some people have found it illuminating and fun to engage with the material in this book with their friends who are also over fifty. Sharing perspectives is always enriching.

Although the material in this book looks specifically at the years between fifty and sixty it can be useful even if you have long since passed through this decade of your life. The experience of crossing that boundary lives in your mind and has set the tone for your experience as an elder. You can think of it as a birth. We may not remember anything of our actual birth, but it is a fairly well accepted psychological axiom that the birth experience can condition the course of a person's perspective in life. On a slightly lesser level this is true for any new stage of life we enter. Our first day in kindergarten sets the stage for how we feel about school. Our fist sexual experience is the cornerstone on which we build later sexual encounters. Our first child gives us the archetypal experience of what it is like to be a parent. Our second child may be different but we will experience that difference in comparison with the first. So it is with the process of becoming an elder. If we look back to the years in which we transitioned from adulthood into elderhood, we will see that this is where we set the tone for our sixties, seventies and much of our eighties. Reflecting on the experiences you had crossing that threshold can only deepen your awareness of what you have learned and how it holds meaning in your life.

So whether you are in your fifties or eighties, welcome to the threshold where things generally only felt are spoken, where we can look with ruthless compassion at who we have been, who we are and who we might become.

Chapter 1

The Language of Astrology

If life is a journey, then it is no surprise that every once in a while we feel the need for some kind of navigational tools. In this book we will approach the transition from adult to elder through the lens of symbolism. The symbols we will use are astrological ones. Even if you have never considered astrological symbolism—what planets and signs might mean, for example—you may know more about these symbols than you realize. I could have written this book without ever mentioning astrological terms, but with more than thirty years of experience practicing astrology, it strikes me that astrology is a most useful and accessible symbolic language.

This need to actively navigate the white waters of life's changes is most pronounced when we stand at the threshold of a major life transition. In the West, we are expected to develop strong and independent identities. In facing life's challenges, each of us is the hero in our own story. When we come to a transition, a time when we must cross a threshold—to become an elder, for example—our intense sense of individuality can also mean that many of us face these major changes feeling as though we are on our own.

Facing the transition to our elder years in the twenty-first century we find ourselves contending with some unique conditions unlike those of our ancestors. Being born is the first major transition of our lives. Second to that we come to adolescence. At this time our bodies changed in ways that would have been familiar to humans for generations before us, but our sexual identity was emerging into a world unlike that of our parents and grandparents. Until the sexual revolution of the late 1960s, many young women were surprised, confused and embarrassed by their first period; they were often left to navigate the ups and downs of the menstrual cycle alone. Although by the last decades of the twentieth century it had become permissible, even accepted, to talk about these things and even joke about them, today's elders emerged from a society that still fostered an environment of shame and secrecy around the transition from child to adult. As they became partners and parents the lack of openness continued; they were often on their own when it came to sustaining a marriage or raising healthy children.

Technology has made such radical changes in the fabric of reality from the time of our parents' coming of age to our own that we have quite literally stepped into a world that is not the same as the one we were born into. Doing things the way your mother or grandmother did made no sense to us as we became adults. This is exciting to think and talk about, but for many of us, it was disorienting to experience. The lack of guidelines contributes to a sense of confusion as to how we might make this transition to our elder years or even if we really have to at all. Like the other great transitions of our lives, it is not well marked or even acknowledged in many cases. We assume that being an adult extends somehow into a period of life called retirement or semi-retirement and then we die. This final stage of life seems in a vague way to be some kind of logical extension of adult life. Yet we all sense that there is a difference between adulthood and what we will call elderhood.

Since the mid twentieth century it has become more and more commonplace to mark our transitions in highly individualistic and creative ways. Everything from graduation to burials has been re-invented. Such is the nature of cultural transformation.

Although it is quite likely that this process is necessary, it also creates confusion as to what is expected of us at various thresholds. Reinventing ourselves is a creative and wonderful process. To reinvent ourselves as elders we must be mindful that this stage of life is distinctly different from adulthood. Growing old is one of the most mundane things about life. We all start out young and, if we are lucky, grow old. Yet each of us experiences aging in a personal way. We are all human—we are all the same—yet in a simple but profound way we are each different. For example, losing a parent is not a generic experience although it happens to most of us. It's *my* mother who dies and in that thought is found the nature of my relationship to her and all that is lost with her passing. I remember my first kiss as if it happened only to *me.* These universal experiences unfold in uniquely powerful ways in our individual lives.

As mentioned in the introduction there is a distinct difference between a sign and a symbol. When we are driving along the road and we see a stop sign, we stop. There is no deeper interpretation required. When we look at the world symbolically we look *through* things, not *at* them. Looking at the Moon or the brilliant light of the planet Venus shining in the western sky after sunset, we may see more than the simple fact of an orb shining in the night sky. Unlike stop signs, shining orbs hanging in the sky excite the imagination, giving us a sense that there is more to life than what is obvious.

The language of symbols can open many doors, enabling us to glimpse the archetypal patterns that underlie existence. These patterns are true for everyone, whether they are perceived to be astrological patterns or are understood in another symbolic language. An archetype is a constellation or pattern of energy. In its pure form, an archetype is invisible to us. We sense archetypal patterns but we cannot see them directly.

To understand archetypes, we must "dress them up" in something. Let's begin with the archetype of the mother. In astrology, this pattern of energy is symbolized by the Moon. We may not know anything about *the* mother but we definitely know about *our* mother. What we know about our personal mother is the door that opens onto the archetype of *the* mother. Astrology gives us a very elegant and ancient language for dressing the archetypes in something that we can then interpret. Think of this "dressing up" as metaphor. Metaphor is the device we use which allows us to see that which is invisible. Poets use it, as do songwriters, filmmakers and novelists. Astrology gives us a way of catching and holding an energy pattern or archetype as it unfolds through time, which allows us to develop a deeper understanding of the nature of our journey through this life.

By using astrology's rich language, we can interpret our experience at all stages of life. The alphabet of astrology consists of the twelve signs, the Sun, Moon, planets and stars and how we perceive them from our place on Earth. Any individual horoscope assumes that the person to whom it belongs is standing at the center of the universe, with everything revolving around that spot, even the Sun and the stars. We have known for hundreds of years that this is not scientifically correct, yet the basic truth stands: each of us must, of necessity, live life as if we are at the center of our experience.

If we think of astrology as a language then each planet and sign can be considered to be a "letter" of the astrological alphabet. As we mix these letters up we get 'words' which then offer a way of contemplating a particular pattern. The horoscope which is cast for a person's birth moment is populated by the Sun, the Moon (which are called luminaries because they are not planets and they light up the sky), the 5 planets which are visible to the naked eye and the 3 outer planets as well as some asteroids and planetoids which require a telescope to be seen. Each of these planets and luminaries is like an actor in the play of a person's life. You may have the Sun in Leo and the Moon in Scorpio but your child or partner may have the Sun in Sagittarius and the Moon in Taurus. There are innumerable ways to combine these symbols and each combination tells a different story—one for each person that has ever lived for that matter.

Astrology offers valuable insight into the symbolic meaning of different stages and thresholds of our lives. You could say that astrological symbolism works on two levels in an individual life. One level speaks to specific qualities and events in our lives. Perhaps all people fall in love at some point but I may have fallen in love for the first time at the age of twelve and you may not have experienced these feelings until you were in your forties. This experience of falling in love for the first time is unique to the individual. The other level at which astrological symbolism communicates to us is what I call the *human continuum.* These are the things that happen to each and every one of us at roughly the same age. So I may fall in love at twelve and you at forty-one, but both of us will lose our baby teeth and begin to get our adult teeth around the age of seven. Interestingly enough, these commonly experienced events on the human continuum are reflected astrologically by planetary movements that happen to everyone at the same age.

An example of this is the Saturn return. Approximately every twenty-nine years Saturn returns to the place it occupied when you were born. This Saturn return happens to everyone at roughly the same age: when you are approximately twenty-nine and again at fifty-eight (and if you live that long, at eighty-seven). Universal experiences are associated with the various thresholds in our lives. This book offers an opportunity to explore the experience of crossing the threshold of the second Saturn return, which I call elderhood. I have noted all the astrological events that we share on the continuum and will use them in this book as a guide for understanding what they are telling us about this fascinating stage of life.

Based on the Saturn return, astrology posits that our elder life lasts about twenty-nine years or until we are approximately the age of eighty-eight. This book is addressed mainly to those who are between the ages of fifty and eighty-eight. At eighty-eight we become what I think of as *living ancestors.* Our minds may be sharp and our bodies spry, but there is no doubt which way we are headed. If we are not frightened by death, this is a time when we can live consciously and with wise acceptance in the world of the living and the world of those who have passed on. Nothing is required of us at this stage other than to offer those younger than ourselves an opportunity to contemplate the amazing power that pulls us into and through life with its passions, joys and sorrows. Whether our lives have been meaningful for us is not the issue at this stage. In a sense we exist for others that they may measure their view of the meaning of life against the living proof of where we all must come.

In psychoanalysis, there is a theory that the experience of birth is also the first moment of anxiety in the life of an individual and can set the tone for the way a person is likely to approach life's challenges. It is quite possible that we bring this pattern of response to all of life's thresholds, including entering our elder years. If we liken this passage to a birth, then it's likely that the awareness we bring to this crossing can significantly color our experience of being elders. At birth, we had no say in the matter. As elders, we can choose to honor the transition.

Human beings have a deep need to find significance in our lives. Using many different tools, we go to great lengths to understand the meaning of events. This book is an exploration of what astrology can teach about becoming an elder and living fully in your new role.

USING THIS BOOK

The older we get the more obvious it becomes that having answers can be limiting but asking questions opens wide the possibilities of understanding. Reading a book such as this might inspire you to write in the margins or try your hand at the exercises in the back of the book. As we become elders we can build bridges from our personal stories, our experiences as individuals, to an awareness of the collective story and experience. In doing this we step back from our lives and gain perspective which leads us to understand life as meaningful both personally and collectively.

Keeping a journal and doing the exercises in the back of this book can enhance your experience of exploring the material. Even if you don't keep a journal however, by reading this material you will have alerted your inner being that something important has happened or is about to. This in itself is a significant improvement over ignoring the whole thing and hoping for the best. You can read this book on your own or with friends. This is up to you and the kind of person that you are. You know what works best for you. I encourage you again to trust yourself.

Should you decide to keep an elder journal know that it is a very personal thing. In a way you are writing to a future part of yourself. When we engage with symbolic reality we enter into a conversation with our inner being. The more we participate, the more it becomes a two-way conversation. Using your writings to note what is most meaningful to you may include your dreams and anything of significance that you discover during the time you are reading the book—whether you understand their relevance at the moment or not. This is a personal discovery, a tool for connecting your inner and sometimes unconscious voice with your conscious life. In no way is this book about simply acquiring more information to stuff into our already over-informed minds. As elders it becomes increasingly important to listen to the still, small voice within. In this way we achieve greater awareness of and deeper meaning in our lives.

As mentioned in the introduction even if you are over sixty and feel you have passed the threshold of elderhood, this book may be useful to you. It is never too late to grapple with the meaning of experience. Understanding a transition even long after you have gone through it can still shed light on the journey. The book you might create for yourself through journaling will emerge from memories and stories of the life you have lived thus far. When the way is not clear, your notes can help validate your experience even when people around you don't seem to understand. It is not only useful to have support in times of difficulty; it can also be helpful to have a witness in times of joy or expanded awareness. Your elder journal can be that witness. In your experience of consciously becoming or being an elder, you will find the perfect wisdom for your needs because you will have defined elderhood for yourself.

As you read the different segments of this book you will find examples of three women on the journey of being or becoming elders. Using their personal stories helped me to develop some of the more challenging concepts in the book. For those of you who are well versed in astrology, you will find their astrological charts in Appendix I, Chapter 1; however, reading their charts is not necessary to understand the meaning of their life experience.

Our first elder is Esther. She was born on August 18, 1936, in New York City, deep in the heart of the Great Depression. She is the older sister of a younger, favored brother. There was much sibling rivalry. She attended Julliard School of Music but was never a professional musician, although she did perform at times. She was married in her twenties, divorced in her thirties and never had children. In her early 30s she became ill and, eventually was diagnosed with breast cancer. Rather than relying solely on her doctors, after becoming ill she adopted a strict vegetarian diet and daily yoga to survive the cancer and regain her strength following radiation and chemotherapy.

Our next elder is Linda, who was born in Vancouver on May 12, 1947. Linda was raised by an alcoholic father with a troubled past and a bad temper and a mother who was distant but tried to hold the family together. Although her mother kept it to herself, it was obvious to Linda that her mother felt easily wronged. Linda is the third of four children. She was academically gifted and graduated from university. In her mid-twenties she married a man who was abusive like her father. He was not an alcoholic but had a bad temper and made it difficult for her to enjoy life. They had two children, but divorced when the children were young. She raised them on her own. She is a well-respected social worker and therapist. Over the years she has combined her psychological insights with expressive therapies such as psychodrama. She has not remarried.

Kate is the youngest of the three. She was born on November 15, 1960 in Toronto, the second of four children. She is from a good family with high standards. Her parents were hard working professionals with high expectations of what their children should accomplish. Kate married a challenging but devoted and interesting partner in her mid 20s. He likes the way she runs their lives. Kate has a degree in business and two children. She is very ambitious and very successful. She likes to be in control of her life. Getting older to her seems like a task. She intends to read up, figure it out and do it right. At around the age of 40 she left her structured career and is a consultant who runs her own business.

Then there is the question of your own astrological chart. Each symbolic piece that we use will resonate with you whether or not you have the exact information which can be known from your birth chart. For example, you may not know your Moon sign but you definitely know a lot about your relationship with your mother. By using your sense of the quality of that relationship you can choose which astrological symbol most closely evokes it. Or you can just bypass the astrological framework all together. At the back of this book in Appendix I you will find a list of keywords. It might be useful to copy them so you can have them at the ready when you want to use them. One thing is certain, whether you use the keywords or trust your own interpretation of your life, you can't go wrong. Keywords are like dream images. They inevitably point to realities other than themselves.

If you would like a copy of your birth chart, notated for the exercises in this book, please send your time, date and location of birth with a cheque for $15.00 US or Canadian to: Julie Simmons, 1562 Danforth Ave., P.O. Box 72089 Toronto, ON, Canada M4J 5C1.

The basic information we are using in this book can be found in the birth chart of each and every person on the planet. This is a snapshot of the solar system as seen from the perspective of earth. As I said previously, an astrological chart is cast as if the person is at the center of the solar system as well as the universe itself. We know that the Sun, Moon and stars do not revolve around the earth but that is not how it appears to us. When we look to the east in the early morning and we see the sky getting lighter we do not say, "The earth is turning." We say, "The sun is rising." How things appear to us lies at the very heart of how we live our lives. An individual's astrological chart gives us insight into how the world appears to the individual to whom it belongs.

Chapter 2

Laying the Groundwork

By the time you turn fifty you have come a long way. Somehow you have survived the dangers of infancy, the dark whirlpool of adolescence, the searching of the twenties, the demands of the thirties and the passionate confusion of the forties, and here you stand at the gate to your fifties. In many ways, because you live in a culture which venerates youth, you have a very weak idea of what it means to be this age. As baby boomers have begun to arrive at the threshold of their old age it is true that there are many more images of older women in the media. Although most of these images are an idealized version of how we might look as we age there are also a few that portray a reasonably accurate picture of this stage of life. For those who are younger this is a great benefit. For those of us born before 1970 we have much work to do to create a physical image that we can appreciate as a valid reflection of what we might look like as we age.

Both men and women are challenged by unrealistic images of how it could be for us as we age. We are expected to be trim, physically vigorous and sexually appealing. A dash of white at the temples, a sexy car and the power to run the world are required of men. Women who have fought for their visibility since their twenties have their own version of this which may include the car and the power but every trace of white is better covered over.

Far less accessible are images of the inner landscape of aging. Much is being written about the external circumstances of life from the over sixty perspective. We are aware of the circumstances of our emerging demographic in times of great change. Because the actual experience of these uncharted waters of the elder years is very subjective we gain the most when we are willing to do some spiritual imaging of our lives from within. The information we glean from others must be filtered through our inner voice. Otherwise we will have only a virtual experience of eldering rather than an authentic one. One area where we all have the option of images of elders that might inspire us at the heart level is in the photographs and memories we have of beloved parents or grandparents. Although styles of hair and clothing have changed over years, the feelings that we have towards these elders can be a great inspiration and comfort to us as we age.

No matter whether we are comfortable or not with the image of ourselves as aging, in the privacy of our own minds it is not uncommon to consider the irrational and persistent question, *how could this be happening to me*?

The first astrological event that meets you on the threshold of your fifties is the Chiron return. Although Chiron is not actually a planet it is a heavenly body commonly used by modern astrologers. When you were born it was located at a certain point in your chart. As it travels around the Sun and through the zodiac from our perspective here on earth it will return to the exact place it was in when you were born when you are between the ages of 49 and 51. We call this the Chiron return. As you enter into your 50s you must pass through Chiron's gate; actually, you must spend some time in his cave. Let me explain.

Imagine you are a pilgrim. For a pilgrim the journey unfolds to give you experiences that will enable you to achieve greater awareness. You have traveled far and finally reached your destination. You are filled with a sense of accomplishment as well as trepidation. You know that the end of one journey is inevitably the beginning of another. Chiron, mentor to all, is there to greet you at the mouth of a cave. In the dim light you see that he is not riding a horse, as first you thought; he is a man from the waist up and a horse from the waist down—a centaur. Although he welcomes you with genuine warmth, you can't help but notice that he is wounded in his left shoulder. His pain is palpable but his smile is genuine. You have come a long way. You realize that there is nothing to do but enter Chiron's realm. You have questions about what is expected of you and what you can expect. You are not sure you made this journey willingly and even less sure about what it means. To answer your questions, we need to look at what and who Chiron is.

First we will deal with the *what.* Chiron is a relatively recent member of the astrological pantheon. One of the ways astrologers build a picture that suggests the symbolism of a heavenly body is to study its physical characteristics. In this way we can begin to interpret its meaning. Chiron was first discovered in 1977 and has fascinated astrologers ever since. It has been classified as a planetoid, a comet and an asteroid. Apparently it originates in a place called the Kuiper Belt, which is located in the far reaches of our solar system. For our symbolic purposes, what is interesting about Chiron is that although it comes from the edges of deep space it has an orbit that is so extreme it seems to *gallop* through the solar system. In one approximately fifty-year cycle it spends about one third of its time inside the orbit of Saturn, and the rest of its time outside and beyond. In short, it travels. Given this fact it is easy to see why this heavenly body was named Chiron the Centaur. Following the *as above, so below* philosophy that underpins astrological thinking, once we have decided that Chiron is a centaur, then we can look for symbolism in his mythological story to help us understand the meaning of entering into our 50s.

THE MYTH OF CHIRON

One day Cronos caught sight of the beautiful nymph Philyra and decided to pursue her. To escape, Philyra turned herself into a mare and galloped away as fast as she could, but Cronos turned himself into a stallion and forced himself upon her. Thus was Chiron conceived. He was born with the body and legs of a horse and the torso and arms of a man. Philyra was so revolted by the sight of him that she turned into a linden tree. Abandoned by his mother, Chiron was raised by Apollo. Apollo stands for "all in Greek character and life which we think of as civilization."[1] Unlike other centaurs, Chiron was immortal. And as Apollo's foster son, he grew up to be wise beyond measure. Chiron was the mentor of heroes, artists, musicians, healers and oracles. Where we find him in our astrological charts, we will undoubtedly learn a lot, as he represents the wise teacher (see Appendix I).

For thousands of years before the discovery of Chiron the symbolism of the centaur was interpreted through the constellation of Sagittarius which is depicted by a centaur with a bow and arrow in his hands. The arrow loosed from the bow is a symbolic indication of vision which reaches far and wide. To be a good teacher one must have vision. In modern times the centaur is also associated with the Southern Hemisphere constellation Centaurus where he still carries his bow and arrow.

Chiron is also a manifestation of the wounded healer. One of Chiron's most famous students was Hercules. One day as Chiron was teaching Hercules how to shoot a poisoned arrow, Hercules accidentally hit Chiron in the left shoulder. Since Chiron was immortal, he did not die; because he had made the poison himself from the blood of the Hydra, he knew for certain that there was no antidote. Wounded by his own poisoned arrow, Chiron was unable to help himself. Thus the wounded healer is doomed to suffer. Because Chiron is also the wise teacher, we suspect that he learned many things about the nature of suffering even as he experienced his own. Perhaps this was his greatest teaching.

Chiron suffered for many years, maybe more than a lifetime in our perception, until Hercules found a way to help him. Hercules convinced Zeus to free Prometheus in exchange for Chiron's death. (Prometheus was being punished for giving fire to mortals.) This switch freed them both—Chiron was able to die, and Prometheus gained his freedom.

As stated above when you are between the ages of forty-nine and fifty-one, Chiron returns to the place it was when you were born. At this time in our lives we all come symbolically to Chiron's cave and he offers us a great teaching about what it means to suffer by our own hand. When we experience painful or difficult times in our lives it often feels that these things happened to us. We tell ourselves that 'if only' this person hadn't done that thing or if this event hadn't happened the way it did then life would be different. Of course it is true that things happen one way and if they had happened another life would be different. It is also true that the amount of suffering we experience regarding things that have happened to us is greater or less depending on how we think about it. One person never recovers from the fact that her husband betrayed her. Another understands that her husband's betrayal and the subsequent pain it brought was an event that woke her up and showed her significant truths about who she truly is. The Chiron Return suggests a time of reflection on our relationship to the wounds that don't heal. Just as Chiron had to live with his poisoned shoulder we have issues and situations that don't resolve. Through this reflection we open the possibility of a deeper awareness of the gift that suffering may bring.

Chiron shows us a few things. First, there is the amazingly liberating yet sobering awareness that many of the wounds that we carry cannot be fixed. The Chiron Return arrives at a time when we have lived long enough to realize that some things can't change. We may have regrets about choices we made, but what is certain is that for some reason we don't understand or can't condone we made those choices ourselves. The Chiron Return encourages us to seek our ancient, inner wisdom and to acknowledge the possibility that our suffering may not need to be fixed. Instead, we can use it to gain a deeper understanding of the nature of our individual experience as well as the nature of life itself. From this powerful teaching sprouts the seeds of compassion.

As we explore this territory, we discover that much of our suffering is self-inflicted. It is one thing to suffer on account of someone else's bad behavior and another to spend your time and energy telling yourself that it could or should have been different. The impulse to obsessively return to situations that caused us to suffer is something we do to ourselves. In his death Chiron shows us that to alleviate suffering we must be able to die. Metaphorically, this suggests suggest two things. One is that we must let the past die if we are to move on, the other that we are freed from our suffering to the extent that we can accept the inevitability of our own death. This helps us to let go of our ego's denial. Only when we let go of the ego's drive to live forever can we be free to actually live fully in the present. One of the most powerful ways the ego holds onto power is through identification with its own suffering. The gift we find in Chiron's cave is this: What we can't fix shows us our true nature and the nature of reality itself, if we let it. By even entertaining the notion that suffering is our teacher we may, over time, be liberated from much of our past suffering just as Chiron liberated Prometheus.

By the time Esther had her Chiron Return, she had done a considerable amount of therapy (see Appendix I). One of the most painful issues in her life was her difficult relationship with her brother. Because Esther had no children she would have liked to be close to his. As much as Esther wanted this he held her at a distance and at her Chiron Return she lost the will to keep trying to connect. Painful as it was, this understanding allowed her to reach into her community and involve herself in the lives of children of her friends. Although she could not resolve her relationship with her brother, she accepted the powerful truth of how damaging early sibling rivalry had been in her family. This newfound compassion made her more sensitive and available to the children she was actually close to. Previously, she had often favored one child over another in families she knew. As Esther reviewed the situation in her family she realized that throughout her life she was hurt by the fact that her brother was the favored child. She came to understand the many ways in which she had bullied him to get him to see that he wasn't better than she was. She even came to realize that her over-striving was even to this day a result of wanting to be better than her brother. The fact that he had children and she didn't seemed to prove in some way that he was better than she was. It was as if God had blessed him and not her. She came to understand how her brother might have wanted to keep her away from his children based on the past dynamic between them. She saw clearly and for the first time that the only power she had to change this pattern with her brother was simply to see it. Once this was clear she cultivated within herself the ability to love each of her friends' children equally if differently.

At the time of our Chiron Return we are often struck with a sense that the story we have told ourselves and others about our life is a metaphor, a personal myth or legend. It is as if we had a dream about what happened, one we can describe by rote. I have often heard people who are dating in their fifties complain about having to "tell their story" over and over to each new person they meet. It can feel a bit stale and yet, like the Ancient Mariner in the poem by Samuel Taylor Coleridge [2], we are somehow compelled to tell and retell our story until we, like he, can find the wisdom that comes from difficult events which we create of our own volition.

The Chiron Return indicates that the time has come not to tell the story by rote, not to use it to explain our failures and successes, but to interpret it from a new perspective, one that appreciates the wisdom it offers, not just the pain. The way we understand ourselves at fifty can open the door from a limited, personal and isolating sense of who we are to an expansive, universal and more inclusive awareness of ourselves. We begin to have a greater perspective on our story, maybe just because we have lived for fifty years. We are perhaps interested in the awareness that everyone without exception has a story that is as compelling to them as ours is to us. We begin to glimpse the profound, universal truth that each person's story is not just about the details of that story but a way to learn about the nature of being human, not just about who we are as individuals. The fact that our story is one of many stories connects us to the world in a way that can make us wiser and more compassionate. Esther understands that there is a great lesson in approaching her sense of alienation from her brother and his family by connecting to her friends' children. In the end this turns her toward a more insightful understanding of the early childhood dynamics between her and her brother which is useful in understanding herself. Although it seems impossible to resolve this with him due to the lack of sympathy they have had for one another over their lives she herself moves toward inner resolution of this painful situation. Even more significant, however, is the ability that begins to grow within her that she can make a difference in the dynamics of sibling relationships of the children she comes to love and perhaps help prevent the kind of difficulty she has grown up with.

For Linda the wisdom she gained at her Chiron Return was an understanding of how the anger she felt at being manipulated and abused by her father's alcoholic behavior had become part of who she was. What began to dawn on her was that there is actually a difference between rage and anger. Her visceral memory of what it was like when her father's drinking made him a towering, dangerous bully to her mother as well as the children would rise up inside her as an adult in her intimate relationships at the slightest hint of aggression. Her father had a way of slurring his speech and bellowing at the same time that would send Linda into an anxiety attack. The feeling of powerlessness in the face of such mindless and unpredictable aggression that she had felt as a child would take her over at times as an adult. Her reaction was to fight against it by hurling her own rage at her partner when provoked by his behavior even if it wasn't happening on account of a drunken, alcoholic stupor. Her sense of betrayal in her marriage was justifiably anger-producing, but it wasn't until she had a much more minor relationship in her mid forties that she began to realize how her rage was something that made her sick and was more about her anxiety level than the behavior of her partner. She had been dating a man for a few months. Suddenly, one day he called her up and professed his love for her. By the end of the conversation he was telling her how he wanted to move in with her and the children and share her life. Linda wasn't in love with him and suspected that he was professing his love for her more out of need than a genuine feeling of love. She said nothing at the time but she knew she didn't want to continue the relationship. A week later when he forgot an important date that they had she became irrationally enraged at him. She tells how she blew him away with a kind of meanness that she didn't know she had. This ended the relationship for which Linda was glad but in retrospect she realized that she could have told him she wanted to end it in a much less aggressive way. Because he hadn't actually bullied her with his manipulations she could see clearly that she had acted the bully. Slowly but surely through this experience her perspective on who she was in relationships began to change. Although she has had many relationships with men they have most often ended in rage, blame and total rejection. By the time she came to her Chiron Return she could see how she had helped to create these scenarios because of a subconscious need to avenge the suffering of her childhood. As she began to separate her anger from rage, two things happened. She no longer had a compulsive need to be in a relationship, and she was able to feel compassion for herself around the intense anxiety she had always felt in intimate relationships with men.

When Chiron opens the door it is wise to enter.

(For an exercise pertaining to the Chiron return, see Appendix II: Chiron Exercise)

DURGA

When women friends of mine turn fifty, I give them a statue of the Hindu goddess Durga along with the story of her deeds.

Although Durga is not a planet or an astrological symbol, her story speaks to the growing awareness that our personal story is also the story of the world. As China Galland wrote in *The Bond Between Women*, Durga teaches us about "fierce compassion," about "transforming anger into compassion."[3] Durga's story "tells us the divine feminine will rise up when the world is in danger, that help comes from forgotten quarters—from what's been cast out, lost, rejected and marginalized, and that what we have cast out is what saves us, what becomes the cornerstone for a new foundation."[4] Here is her story.

THE STORY OF DURGA

"The world stood poised on the brink of destruction once before.

Rivers dried up, plants did not grow. People starved. War was everywhere. Slaughter prevailed. Dancing stopped, even singing was forgotten. The demons . . . raged unchecked across heaven and earth, drunk on destruction. No one could stop them, not even the gods, who had been defeated, one by one.

Humiliated, the gods withdrew to the heights of the Himalayas and took counsel amongst themselves. Their situation seemed hopeless. They had lost all power against these demons and could only leave the world to its inevitable destruction. Then it was remembered that this time had been foretold—a demon would come to destroy the world, and only a woman could defeat this demon—only a woman could save the world." [5]

Out of the maelstrom came the great goddess Durga, "blazing with the light of a thousand suns, radiating her splendor throughout the universe. Riding a lion, wearing the crescent Moon, smiling serenely, Durga had ten arms, powerful and ready with weapons given to her by the gods themselves". [6]

Durga battled the great demons for days on end. The earth and its oceans and mountains heaved and roiled. As Durga battled, fierce and focused legions of female warriors came into being to fight by her side. Demons were slain and bodies fell on both sides. In the end Durga and her forces were victorious.

However, as often happens when battling a demonic force, victory was short lived. Each time they rose up, no matter what form they took, Durga always prevailed. Eventually, the demons changed their approach. They tried to seduce Durga with an offer of marriage. But she had taken a vow that she would only marry the one who could defeat her in battle.

Eventually, Durga became so enraged by the demons' refusal to accept defeat that, 'Her face grew as dark as a storm cloud, and the Goddess Kali sprang full-blown from her forehead—armed, black, enormous, terrifying, and ready for battle'. [7]

Kali was a dreadful sight as she stepped out onto the battlefield. She filled the heavens and earth with her horrifying cry as she devoured the demon forces.

Finally only one demon remained. This one challenged Durga to fight him alone without the help of Kali and her female warriors.

Durga absorbed Kali and all her female warriors back into herself. Alone, she rode on to the battlefield astride her lion. The struggle for the fate of the world began.

Time stopped as goddess and demon battled. The entire cosmos twisted at the vast power of their encounter. But once again, Durga prevailed, piercing the demon with a dagger through the heart.

"The world was safe at last.

A great cry of victory rang out across the world. All the gods assembled to honor Durga and to crown her Queen of the Universe. Rivers returned to their courses; music, dance and song returned to the world. Plants grew, trees blossomed, joy could be found again. The earth itself seemed to rejoice". The gods begged her to stay and although she refused as she withdrew from the world she made a promise: "Do not worry. If the world is ever in danger of being destroyed again, I will return." [8]

We cannot become conscious elders in times of chaos if we don't face the world's pain. The suffering of the world is a significant part of our elder years. Who is not touched by the poverty, violence, destruction and disease that overwhelm the world in these times? Our personal pain is a lens through which we encounter the pain of the world. "There is a goodness, a wisdom that arises . . . from within us, like the force that drives green shoots to break the winter ground . . . into that part of ourselves that can never be defiled, defeated or destroyed, but that comes back to live, time and time again, that lives—always—that does not die."[9]

As women enter their fifties, menopause can play havoc with the mental, emotional and physical bodies. The sense of destruction occurring simultaneously in your inner world and the outer world can be overwhelming. Durga's story reminds us that this is not the first time the world has stood on the brink of extinction. This is not the first time that powerful and overwhelming negative energies have threatened everything we hold dear. Just as Durga comes out of hiding to save the world from destruction each of us has the potential to return to our awareness the parts of us that have been cast out and forgotten from childhood. Because we have lived for fifty odd years on this planet we can sort through our behaviors and experiences from the past with some perspective. Through this process of reuniting ourselves with aspects of our own psyche that we have disowned due to misunderstanding or shame we, like Durga, have the ability to defeat the forces that threaten to overwhelm us.

Through understanding her rage Linda not only has the possibility of an intimate relationship but she also has a deeper understanding of the rage and anxiety of the women she works with. Esther's understanding of the pain and destruction which sibling rivalry brings to families ripples out into her community. This newfound power of the feminine to integrate the past with the present which naturally begins to occur as we enter our fifties can transform the world both personally and collectively.

Kate is just beginning to experience her Chiron return at this writing, the issue of becoming an elder in times of 'economic downturn' and who-knows-what-else, the sense that her very efficient and well-managed life may be derailed by other people's bad judgment has thrown her into an exploration of what value all her efforts will have in the long run. She is quite literally involved in an exploration of her values as she enters this stage of life. Like Durga she has no doubt that she will crack the code of this crises and save, at the least, her world if that is what is called for.

The notion that there is a fierce power within us that can transform and heal—which we each must claim for ourselves—speaks to women directly. It also suggests that these same qualities in men that have been cast out and denied, if brought to consciousness, could transform the world.

In considering Durga at this time we deepen our understanding of what Chiron's Return is about. There is something they have in common. As we enter the realm of our fifties in the late twentieth and early twenty-first century, it is clear that the world we have known and lived in is being destroyed and transformed. In these times of chaos, this is true in both a personal and global sense. As you pass through the gates of your early fifties you have the opportunity to meet your inner shaman, that aspect of yourself that can teach you the value of your suffering and the mystery that lives at its core. You are in some sense an old adult at the threshold of becoming a young elder. Perhaps you are filled with a sense of relief that you don't have to fix yourself. In fact, you realize that you aren't broken! What you are required to do from here on is to live your life fully, recognizing and accepting your wounds in the ways that they have shaped you and doing the best you can to save what can be saved in this chaotic world. We are in need of Chiron's wisdom which comes from personal suffering as well as Durga's courage and strength to deal with the world now more than ever.

Between the beginning and middle of your fifties, there are other astrological events which occur for everyone along the human continuum. Now that we know we don't need to be fixed, it becomes possible to deepen our sense of who we are emotionally, intellectually, spiritually and psychologically. Working through these astrological events (described below) helps to lay a strong foundation for the journey to elderhood. If you are to find any kind of genuine stability, you must begin to cultivate the ability to look within and *know thyself* as the ancient Greek aphorism commands us to do. Some say that the fifties are the *divine decade,* and perhaps that is because we begin to cultivate the qualities of inner searching and spiritual development. This can be a blessing if we are willing to see it as such.

Chiron has opened the door, Durga has suggested the need for fierce compassion and now you must anchor yourself on the shifting sands of the world as it is. As you journey on, keep in mind that you are living the experience of becoming an elder in a world fraught with chaotic transformation. If we aren't in denial, there is bound to be tension between our instinct to accept life as it is and the feeling that acceptance might mean capitulation to the destruction of our species if not our planet. It is difficult to measure our own needs as individuals against the power of the events that unfold in the world. Some people have a harder time with this than others, to be sure. Here are some suggestions for where to look for a foundation to carry you through the realm of elderhood.

THE FOUNDATION: KNOW THYSELF

This section, the foundation, will relate astrological events involving the Moon, and the three outer planets; Uranus, Neptune and Pluto to the first half of our fifties.

Consider the Moon. No matter what is happening down here where we live, be it war or famine, marriage or birth, love or money, the Moon is always there; the closest heavenly body to our planet, she waxes and wanes with reliability. The Moon pulls the tides; without this ebb and flow there would be no life on earth. Simply put on a symbolic level, she is our mother. Astrologically speaking, the Moon represents the things we learn from our mother, for better or worse, about how to get our needs met. We learn from the way we are conditioned by her how to adjust our circumstances from moment to moment that we may survive as comfortably as possible. The Moon then becomes the symbol for our basic emotional nature. Astrologically speaking the Moon returns to the place it held at your birth in your mid twenties and again in your mid fifties. By tracking these returns we can learn something of our original emotional make-up.

The placement of the Moon when you were born is a description of how you react emotionally to life. It suggests the qualities in your mother with which you resonate most intensely. The Moon is not necessarily how your mother would say she sees you; it's more about how you react emotionally to life based on the way you experienced her. In your fifties and maybe not a moment sooner, you are ready to understand that no matter what kind of mother you had, you reacted to her according to your own nature which can be described by the placement of the Moon in your chart. We have all noticed—either in our own family or in a family close to us—how different children of the same mother may give very different descriptions of who she was and what motivated her actions. From an astrological perspective, it is likely that each of these children has a different Moon placement. Our mothers don't make us who we are; rather, they bring out our basic nature in this way or that, depending on how they treat us. Understanding the basic nature of our emotions can liberate us from the endless loop of blaming our mothers for how we can't get what we need. To understand the Moon's return in our fifties it is useful to look back at our twenties when it first returned.

Until the first return of the Moon in our mid-twenties we are essentially conditioned to react emotionally in a certain way. At the first return of the Moon we leave the transitional realm of our early twenties, which takes us out of childhood, and we begin tentatively to enter adult life. Our emotional resonance mechanism is essentially set by this time, and we may spend the next twenty-five odd years acting more or less the way in which we were conditioned. The second time the Moon returns to its natal position, around the age of fifty-four we have begun the process of leaving our adult life. Menopause has come and perhaps gone, and the impulse to act according to our conditioning is subtly transforming into a sense of acceptance of our emotional nature. At this time it serves us to be honest about what our needs are and perhaps have always been. In our adult life we generally still believe that someone else can meet our emotional needs. We are often caught up in meeting the emotional needs of others to such an extent that we don't have time to consider the true nature of our own emotions. In our fifties this begins to change. Our children and partners don't necessarily want us to change, and we may even wish to go on as always, but somehow we find that some automatic impulses are not what they used to be.

It seems possible that as a woman's body produces less estrogens and testosterone levels rise, we encounter the radical inclination to respond less automatically to the needs of others. According to Leonard Shlain:

> The relative rise in her testosterone levels also brings about dramatic changes in a woman's psyche . . . The indecision, pliability, and relative vagueness of purpose that often marks a woman's youth are replaced by clearheaded assertiveness. Researchers have demonstrated in many different studies that the more testosterone an animal has, the farther away he or she is willing to roam and the more likely he or she will be to challenge and/or dominate a rival. In general, the menopausal jolt of testosterone focuses women on life goals and fills them with a resolve that was often lacking earlier in their lives. [10]

We are entering a period when we can actually be more thoughtful about our emotions. The Moon's return underscores our habitual response to getting (or not getting) what we need. It challenges us to accept ourselves as our mother's child. It is a time when we may catch ourselves in the act of, for example, needing to be needed rather than simply unconsciously acting out one more time. This ability to see ourselves doing the thing we do and have always done is the dawning of a new kind of consciousness. As we pay attention to the mechanism of how we get our needs met we become aware of our habitual behaviors. This is the beginning of a change that will become more and more valuable to us as we become elders.

When we are actually children the astrological Moon suggests the way we experience our mother. As we grow beyond childhood the Moon becomes a symbol for our inner child. The inner child is created and conditioned from the experiences of childhood. The Moon represents the part of us that wants comfort. It shows us how we would like others to comfort us as well as what causes us to feel discomfort. By the time we are fifty-four we are called to see this inner child for who she is; to love her as she is; to understand that she is just who she is. This is definitely not the same as letting her run your life.

As older adults headed down the road to becoming young elders, we may not feel as compelled as we once were to struggle with trying to get people to give us what we think we need to feel comforted. There is a futility to this kind of manipulation. As elders-in-the-making we can strive to make ourselves more comfortable by choosing how and with whom we spend our time and energy. We begin to realize that simply making ourselves comfortable robs us of the edge we need to become more fully awake. Maybe our mothers weren't all that wise about how they met our needs, but at this point and from here on in it makes more sense to figure out how to live with our conditioned responses without having them run our lives. As we become more accepting of our emotional nature being just what it is we have less need to ignore or suppress it, in fact, seeing our conditioning for the programming it is can be a very interesting exercise. This fits in with Chiron's message. We are not broken; we were just made in one image rather than another.

One way to gain insight into the nature of your Moon is to consider what you were going through at your first Moon return. If you look back at your life between the ages of twenty-five and twenty-seven you might recall how in some way literally or perhaps metaphorically you might have returned home to your family for one last round of being a child. By the time you were twenty-seven most likely you had finally set sail into your own life. Understanding who we were at the first return of the Moon can offers insight into the person we are becoming at the second return. (For an exercise pertaining to the Moon's return, see Appendix II: Moon Return Exercise)

When Esther was fifty-four she began playing the piano again after a long absence. At first she was obsessed and spent hours a day in rigorous practice. She even considered performing. Although she was proud to realize that she still had it in her to practice with such dedication, eventually she realized that the obsessive drive to excel was an attempt to be so good that her mother would have to love her. The day this realization hit her it was as if someone had told her the funniest joke of her life. She laughed and laughed. After that her aspirations weren't to perform at Carnegie Hall but rather to invite friends over to hear her pieces. She even began to compose simple songs, which she would give as gifts. On her piano was a small picture of her mother.

For Linda the issue at this stage was about a good friend of hers who needed advice that would make or break her life; or so it seemed. This friend relied heavily on Linda for her insight and loyal friendship. Linda enjoyed the friendship because they had been friends for so long they felt like family. As Linda's friend's problems became more intense, Linda began to realize that she felt oppressed by having to come up with the right answer. Although she enjoyed the almost daily conversations with her friend, she began to back away and look at the dynamic in a different way. Being of a psychological bent anyway it became obvious to Linda that she was exhausted from trying to help her friend, despite how much she loved her. Linda recognized the feeling she had listening to her friend as similar to the feelings she used to have as a child when her mother would tell Linda her problems and Linda couldn't figure out how to help her at all. Realizing that she was repeating a pattern she didn't enjoy Linda stopped trying to help so much and simply offered to listen with a loving heart and an open mind when she had the energy for it. She was pleased to discover that she could have a loyal and loving friendship without exhausting herself. She was then free to genuinely appreciate her friend's ability to find her own solutions to her problems.

When Kate considers her relationship with her mother she sees the high expectations that her mother had for her. She is aware that she strives in a way that most people don't even consider. She looks back to her mid to late 20s and realizes how she was driven to have it all: career, family, success and a happy marriage. The only time she really wonders about this impulse which propels her toward success is when she is physically exhausted—which doesn't happen often. It will be interesting to see how this feels to her through her 50s when the body goes through so many changes.

It is often true that people look back at their lives and acknowledge that some of their greatest awakenings came through difficult times. Despite this it is natural for most of us to avoid suffering and seek pleasure. By the time we are fifty it has become clear that try as we might we cannot be totally in control of our circumstances. Life happens to everyone. We cannot prevent things from happening to us that we don't like and wouldn't choose. As elders we are ready to consider that much of what we think of as suffering comes more through our mental attitude than through the specific circumstances. We all know that generally speaking, things could be worse, yet we can still be more or less miserable depending on how we think about our situation.

As the Moon's return encourages us to accept and consider our emotional nature in our early fifties, so too do the three outer planets offer an empowerment that encourages us to reflect on the nature of our spiritual, intellectual and profoundly human qualities. Although we each experience this through the specific events of our lives, we have the opportunity during the first half of our fifties to actually understand something of the nature of all existence by digging deeper into our own personal nature. A possible positive side effect of becoming an elder in times of chaos is the awareness that anyone and everyone can be touched by the chaos. One person may go bankrupt and another may not but we are all experiencing in a specific way a phenomenon that touches us all. We are separate and yet we are all part of the whole. In this way we may grow in wisdom.

Uranus, Neptune and Pluto are the three planets of our solar system that astrologers typically use [11] that are outside the realm of visibility to the naked eye. They are referred to as the outer planets, and they are associated with what astrologers call the transpersonal realm. We see them as influencing general cultural trends that sweep individuals along rather than specific individual characteristics or events. For thousands of years human beings studied the movements of the planets that they could see on a clear night with the naked eye. As technology became part of the human experience we began to observe these more distant and elusive heavenly bodies. The astrological interpretation of these planets as transpersonal comes from the awareness that for all those thousands of years when we couldn't see the planets they were still out there having an effect. Another reason the outer planets have come to represent cultural change more than personal change is because they move so slowly through the heavens, which means they spend a relatively long time in each sign that they inhabit. They signify something about the generation of which you are a part. Because they move so slowly through the zodiac, people close to you in age will share the effects of the influence of these planets. [12] These planets represent principles of change and transformation over which we feel we have no power as individuals. They might represent such forces as globalization or, on a more personal note, things that happen in our lives which radically alter them: death and destruction, job losses and crop failures, great revelations or revolutions, fashion trends, the zeitgeist—things over which the ego feels powerless.

When the influences of Uranus, Neptune and Pluto enter our lives, change is in the wind. The promise of greater awareness is always implicit, as is the requisite discomfort that inevitably accompanies change. In the first half of our fifties these three planets have a unique way of touching our consciousness. To understand this we will look back for a moment to our late thirties and early forties—the time of mid-life crises. [13]

At this period in our lives we grappled with these same planets and the principles that they represent. We were challenged to become aware of our habitual behavior, to realize that the possibly brilliant survival mechanism we created to cope with our childhood was no longer appropriate to the person we had become. This is what lies at the bottom of the incredible stresses that many people experience in mid-life. In the first half of your fifties, each of these transpersonal planets makes a supportive or empowering aspect to the place it was in when you were born. [14] Because each of these planets is so powerful in its own right, the fact that they all do the same thing at roughly the same time for everyone is symbolically very significant.

When these planets challenge us we know that change is inevitable. We fear it, we try and run from it, but sooner or later we deal with the issues they raise, and if we are lucky we are awakened a bit in the process. When these planets empower us, as they do in our early fifties, they offer us a great gift, which goes something like this: Although it is true that suffering generally gives you push to create awareness, at this period the challenge is about being who you really are without being forced to go there on account of suffering. How hard can that be? The opportunity in the first part of our fifties is a radical kind of acceptance of who we are in relation to our generation and to the culture in general. For some of us—especially middle-class westerners—empowerment is nothing new. We feel a general sense of empowerment and privilege compared to the rest of the world. Western society enjoys a level of material ease that has fostered within us an unconscious belief that we are so blessed with food, shelter, clothing, health care, recreational options and art because we deserve it. Many of us also believe that the rest of the world should live at a comparable level; nonetheless we live our lives enveloped in a cloud of privilege. As the world in general gets more and more chaotic we may take this less and less for granted but so far our sense of entitlement is going strong. We have the option of going through this period in our early fifties unconsciously with the assumption that we are empowered because we deserve it. This rather inflated perspective weakens the foundation for later years when changes in our bodies and the way people see us can bring about feelings of disempowerment. Old age is a great leveler.

People in their early fifties can struggle with difficult issues: divorce, illness, anxiety and financial crises don't vanish just because we have reached a certain age. When difficult things happen in the early fifties we look for astrological indications in the part of the horoscope that isn't along the continuum. We know that the Chiron return encourages us to look at our difficulties as if they are teachings which can make us wiser. The aspects from the outer planets encourage us to use the intellectual, spiritual and psychological foundations we have no matter what events we meet in these years. At this period we are naturally prone to seeing and accepting ourselves in these ways. This is one of those periods in life when we can abide by the old saw that says, 'What doesn't kill you makes you stronger.'

As you come to this period of your life in a world where change and chaos are becoming the norm there are risks to simply resting on a sense of entitlement which arises out of the fact that you are a well fed, well read, relatively healthy person. Surely this may be true in the moment but change is the one thing we can count on—especially as we become elders. A better choice for our chaotic times is to use this period of relative strength to lay a stronger foundation for the future, one that will undoubtedly be quite unlike the past. Remember, it is not necessarily in our nature to reach for the edge when we are comfortable.

Remember also that even if we are relatively comfortable in our individual lives, we are living in times of great chaos. Underlying our sense of security is anxiety about a future that can hardly be imagined. Sometimes we are not even certain that we have a future as a species. What we are working toward in this section is encouragement to reach for the edge of your empowered self. By acknowledging your intellectual, spiritual and psychological strengths you may challenge yourself from within. This will create greater awareness of your strengths which will come in handy as you journey onward in the realm of elderhood and encounter the whirlpools and thunderstorms which lie ahead. In so doing you lay a strong foundation for your elder years.

Empowerment is a wonderful thing when it aligns with greater awareness. Most likely we are not here on this planet, in this life, to be happy simply in the material sense. That kind of happiness is too ephemeral in a world where change is the only constant. Perhaps a more lasting kind of happiness is found when we cultivate greater awareness of the way things actually are rather than grasping at how this moment could be endlessly better if only we had or did something. Greater awareness is not generally found on a path of contented acceptance or desperate grasping but rather through cultivation of a willingness to see things as they truly are. (Not what we are manipulated to see, not what we wish to see, but what is.) In our early fifties we have the opportunity to cultivate the habit of simple and profound acceptance of ourselves. If this becomes a habit it will be easier to hold steady despite the tension of growing older in an uncertain world. It's enlivening.

If your early fifties are a thing of the past, don't skip over what comes next. It is never too late to grapple with cosmic influences. Greater understanding of these principles which we see through the movements of Uranus (intellectual), Neptune (spiritual) and Pluto (psychological) in our charts is always valuable. When we are working with the notion of expanding awareness, time is not linear. Past, present and future can change places in an instant, especially as we get older.

THINKING OUTSIDE YOUR OWN BOX: URANUS

To the ancient Greeks, Uranus was the original sky god. He fell in love with Gaea, the Earth, and they became the parents of the Titans, the original giants who walked the earth before humans. What this suggests to the symbolically minded is that Uranus comes from above, and that it is a mental and intellectual principle. Uranus was the first of the planets to be discovered with the aid of new technology—the telescope. It was detected around the same time as the great revolutions of the 18th century which was also the era when electricity began to be understood as a force of nature usable to humans. Astrologers see this planet as associated with revolution, revelation, liberation and the quantum change that is required for new systems to form and stabilize. It is often active at the time of major scientific breakthroughs or inventions that change the world. In the lives of individuals it brings the unexpected events that awaken consciousness.

Richard Tarnas in his book *Prometheus the Awakener* [15] suggests that in actuality the qualities of Uranus are very like the mythological character of Prometheus. Prometheus stole fire from the gods and gave it to humans. Prometheus was the first rebel, the first to challenge the authority of the gods over the lives of humans. The ability to control fire was the beginning of all human accomplishments. Our amazing achievements (at least in our own minds) separate us from the rest of the animals. They enable some of us to believe that there are no gods. Adding the symbolism of Prometheus to the interpretation of Uranus helps us to see that Uranus is the principle that inspires us to see things in a different way. It is the different drummer. Uranus can represent our friends or social group because they are the people who share our ideals. It incites us to rebel when necessary and if it is strong in your chart you may often feel like a round peg in a square hole. If this is the case, however, you would rather change the square holes to round than become square yourself.

When you are about age fifty-three Uranus or Prometheus arrives on the scene and whispers in your ear, *these are the people you like, this is the conversation and information that interests you and these are the ones that don't.* It offers a kind of revelation about what makes you unique in the way you think and the things you think about. It suggests a time when you might feel the strength of your ideals and intellectual interests. Suddenly you become aware of how truly interested you were by the conversation concerning local politics or maybe that conversation fell flat but what really inspired you was the unexpected enthusiasm your co-worker expressed for knitting. There are many reasons that people are friends with each other. When it comes to the effects of Uranus we are looking at the kind of friendships that are based on the exchange of ideas and especially our aspirations. In our early fifties we find ourselves evaluating our friendships and social life. People we thought we had something in common with may suddenly seem dull and uninteresting. Quite the opposite is possible as well. We may be drawn to new people who inspire us to think differently. When Prometheus steps into the room there is absolutely no point in fighting the truth. You have arrived at the moment when you are ready to open to new ideas and to be inspired to think outside the box you have grown used to.

When trying to get a feel for what your "box" might be, a little reflection on what your ideals were in your early to mid-twenties will shed some light. Perhaps you idealized the notion of personal freedom and the right to make your own way in the world. For some your ideal in your twenties might have been to have what you want, to choose to spend your time and money on what *you* valued. Freedom of speech, civil rights, living in community are the kinds of ideals that we often engage with in our twenties. These ideals give rise to a way of seeing the world that evolves as we grow older but in our twenties the general tendency is to question the ideals which our family of origin may have aspired to. We are drawn to imagine the possible world we might create for our adult lives. In an underlying way these ideals that were strong in your twenties have helped create the life you live.

We get habituated to the thoughts in our mind over time. Here, at the threshold of your elder years you have the mandate to look at how the ideals that inspired you in your twenties have shaped your life. The ideals of a twenty-year-old may need some refreshment if they are to serve a sixty-year-old because the world has changed and so have you. (For exercises pertaining to Uranus, go to Appendix II: Exercises: Uranus)

When Esther reflects back to her twenties she remembers her radical dream was to live with like-minded people in a community of shared values. To this end she was active in politics for a while. In her fifties it was very important for her to have a social group that enjoyed similar things as she did. Radical politics had somehow transformed into art, good food, and time in nature. By making the connection between her youthful idealism and the calmer mind of her fifties Esther realized that art, good food and nature are all issues that require some political effort as well as simple appreciation if they are to remain alive and assessable to all people.

Linda's youthful idealism was about education. She wanted to learn all she could about how to wake people up to their true potential. The more offbeat her professors the happier she was. Before entering the realm of social work Linda studied to become a teacher with the underlying idea that she would create or help sustain alternative education. As a woman in her fifties employed as a social worker and therapist one of Linda's greatest gifts is helping people see outside the box in which they live—the box that creates and recreates their suffering on a daily basis. Interest in alternative education has shifted toward the latest research on the brain and ancient Buddhist teachings. Her ideal is to challenge the thinking of all her clients. She has tempered her low tolerance for people who won't listen to new ideas and has accepted the less radical task of challenging people slowly, over time to consider thinking about their lives in even slightly different ways. Through the practice of meditation and mindfulness training she has learned from firsthand experience exactly how hard it is to shift one's habitual way of thinking.

Kate remembers her 20s as a time of much personal doubt about whether or not she would ever accomplish all she had in mind. She was tortured a she recalls between getting a law degree or a business one. She was also involved with a young man who was totally outside the realm of what her family would have chosen for her. Although she herself didn't approve of him she was strongly attracted and reasonably sure she wouldn't marry him.

When Uranus stirs in our consciousness we become aware of chaos both within and around us. We become aware of the larger world beset with overpopulation, epidemics, climate change and war. We notice the ineffectual way that these things have been dealt with which makes us aware of the unpredictability of outcomes. We may develop an interest in how chaotic situations may give rise to amazing amounts of very intelligent and interesting possibilities as to how this world might work. Although we are bombarded with frightening information about how bad things are and how perilous existence is, we can, if we choose, take a long view and see that perhaps we are actually in a transition and that all this chaos promises a much needed breakthrough in human consciousness. From this perspective it seems we may not just be doomed to a world of mismanagement, natural disasters and armed conflict. There are alternatives. But, of course, in typical Uranus fashion there are just so many alternatives it's hard to know where to start. The influence of Uranus in the first half of our fifties offers us the opportunity to focus our intellectual identity. We sort through the conversations of our lives and decide we would rather talk about one thing and not so much about another. We look back to our youth and consider what happened to that person we once were and how she, with her strength of conviction led us here, to this thought in this moment of our lives, so many years later. It's a kind of gentle revolution which encourages us to trust our intellect as we open to all the new ideas the world has to offer as it rolls and tumbles through its chaotic transformation. We will meet Uranus again at the beginning of our sixties with the same message in a slightly different form.

THE LONGING: NEPTUNE

In ancient Greek mythology Neptune was god of the sea as well as earthquakes and the thunderous pounding of the hooves of white horses like waves crashing upon the shore. From this jumble of images modern astrologers see Neptune as the principle of confusion, illusion, delusion and ultimately transcendence. Just as we have no idea what may wash up after a storm we may not be quite prepared for the welcome and unwelcome things that wash up in our lives after periods of great loss, confusion and or turbulence which Neptune can bring.

Neptune is a tricky fish so to speak. On one hand it represents the sheer immensity of the human capacity for longing and on the other hand all that comes of that longing. Neptune symbolizes all the confusion, addictive behaviors and difficulty that longing can bring as well as exquisite acts of compassion, beauty and spirituality that arise from human emotions which are generated by these same longings. It symbolizes the yearning for things out of reach. It can be dreamy in nature. It can be like getting lost in a good movie or a dangerous, disorienting fog. At their worst the longings of Neptune become addictions; at their best, longings become mystical experiences and may even be channeled into art. When it speaks to us around the age of fifty-four it says: "This is what you long for. This is how you would like to experience transcendence. This is who you are spiritually. This is what you believe, just because you believe. Not because you have proof." Neptune has nothing to do with religion. It is about the direct experience of what many people call God.

If Neptune can be said to anchor us at all it connects us to the universal human condition of longing in all its aching beauty and terrifying immensity. Neptune offers an especially difficult challenge in a materialistic society. Speaking at the level of cultural generalities, we could say that in a consumer society the ache of a Neptunian longing impels us to buy something, eat something, take something or do something rather than to be still and listen. Rarely are we given images that there is nothing that can or should be done. This should not be mistaken for despair however. Neptune and the sense of "nothing to be done" is not about despair. It is about a kind of emptiness that leads to fullness. It is about the need that all humans have to be still and listen to the still, small voice within. Much more despair is generated through trying to feed a hunger which cannot be satisfied by worldly things than from simply feeling what you feel. The general cultural denial of this principle has sent many individuals toward Buddhist thought and meditation. *Don't Just Do Something, Sit There!* [16] is the wonderful title of a book that encourages a healthy use of Neptunian energy.

At the polar opposite of materialism we have the world of fundamentalism. Neptune is in no better shape in a rigid religious environment where control and punishment are the tools used to suppress the ache in the human soul. Neptune is about flow and as such when we are in its sights we must trust the energy itself to carry us to the place of transcendence. The very nature of longing is transformed if you don't try to get away from it; if you allow yourself to be open to it and explore the longing itself. Difficulty arises because inner journeys are ultimately made alone. The reward is in the experience of oneness, which enables us to know we are connected to the greater whole and that separation is an illusion.

Religion may have a purpose in that it can be a way to hold a community together and, at its best, guide people morally, but when we are in Neptune's realm religion can be seen to divide us from one another because it amplifies our differences from people of other religions. This generally distresses Neptune's instinct for the inter-connectedness of all things. Where it allows for the mystical or ecstatic we find a more comfortable relationship between Neptune and religion. Sufis, Kabbalists, and Christian mystics are all on the Neptunian end of religion.

All three of the transpersonal planetary principles suggest that human development requires us to know who we are outside the bounds of conventional society. It is, of course, impossible to do this without hurting yourself and the ones you love if you aren't securely grounded before you break loose. And no matter how transcendent our awareness, we must all "fetch water and carry wood," as the Buddhist saying goes. As long as we are embodied we must attend to our earthly nature. Even under the powerful influence of Neptune's longing for oneness we go in and out of transcendence, at best.

When we are taken over by a strong longing it may feel like a rogue wave that could drown us if we don't struggle against it. Rather, I see this wave of longing to be a wave that we can learn to ride. If you are filled with a deep sense of yearning and you don't suppress it, if you simply ride with it by allowing yourself to feel it, it has the potential to take you to bliss. The synthetic bliss we feel when we feed our longing with addictive substances is a sad parody of one of the most amazing aspects of a human being—the capacity for oneness and bliss.

Neptunian longings take many different forms. There is always a dash of perfectionism where we find Neptune because longing for oneness is about wanting to be held in perfection. Some of us long for and believe in the possibility of the perfect life. God is in the details. At the transcendent end of the spectrum we are drawn to deep service, at the delusional end we self-medicate and worry endlessly.

For others perfection lies in the search and possible attainment of perfect love. We believe, often with no demonstrable proof, in the ultimately fused relationship of soul mates. At the transcendent end of this issue we find the possibility of deep love, the kind that heals the soul. We also have the notion that through the power of love, beauty and truth are one in the same. We believe with or without proof in the wisdom that love brings despite human failing. At the contracted end of this longing is an irrational belief in the Hollywood ending, the emptiness of serial monogamy, the endless search for perfect love in one partner after another.

Neptune's longings can also express through the need to push further and further the edges of sex, mystery and science. We long to expose the great mysteries of life—birth, sex and death—to the light of day where we can know them. This, of course, is futile. The more we try to expose the mysteries of life to the light of day, the more they retreat to deeper levels, more intricate and difficult to fathom. The transcendent side of this particular version of longing is found in a deep respect for the great mysteries and acceptance of oneself as a part of nature rather than outside it. The mystery of creation is something we live with each and every moment of our lives. Attempting to expose it as if we are outside of it drives it away. We can express these longings through art, poetry, music and even science if we respect that we are one with nature and not separate. [17]

For each and every one of us it is important to stay grounded in three-dimensional reality as we face our lives as elders in an electronic age. The World Wide Web gives us access to "virtual reality" which is real enough that we pay for it, plug into it and let it confuse, confound and sometimes expand our sense of who we are. It is obvious to anyone who experiences stiffness in the joints that sitting for too long with our minds plugged in and our bodies not moving only makes us feel worse.

In the sense that we are laying a foundation in our early fifties for our future life as elders, Neptune offers us the possibility of being at peace with our spiritual nature. Some of us know oneness in the garden, through compassionate service, and when we are creating. Others sit and listen. To build a spiritual foundation we must cultivate the ability to let go and let God (or Nature—whatever you wish to name the cosmic force in the universe) reveal itself to us. Essentially we are in healthy relationship to Neptune when we have forgotten about our individual selves and are carried on the wave of something larger.

As we become elders and our bodies become less supple and more noticeable in their aches and pains, we can become frightened of losing our abilities, frightened ultimately about the inevitable loss of life. This fear contracts us. A strong, healthy connection to the principles that Neptune symbolizes allows us to transcend fear, to expand to the fullness of opening to all that is. (For an exercise pertaining to Neptune, go to Appendix II: Exercises: Neptune.)

Esther's experience of Neptune in her early fifties was expressed in the way she felt called to withdraw into her life and create. For a while she became almost anti-social, seeing each interaction with another person to be an invasion of her inner world. One day, her therapist described a goal in human relations as "swimming like fish through the sea of one another, with the ability to merge and separate intact." Esther was stunned into a realization that her hermit-like attachment to being the alienated artist was a bit of an ego trip, and that finding balance and living that balance would enable her to be more authentically creative as well as human.

Linda has longed relentlessly for a love so true that there could be no doubt of its reality. She has believed, in spite of or perhaps because of her experience, that this ideal love was somehow just out of reach for her but ever so close. One day, while writing in her journal about this very topic, she discovered that she had somehow never in her life doubted that this longing she had was for something real and tangible. Suddenly she was aware that her version of true love was akin to a Hollywood movie complete with a *happily ever after* quality. She realized that she couldn't think of even one movie that actually depicted the happily ever after scenario that she so passionately believed in. For one thing it would be boring to watch and for another she, more than most, had observed and experienced the opposite, time and time again. Not only was this a stunning revelation about true love it was also deeply insightful regarding the fact that she could hold so tightly to something that had no substance for so long. As Liz Greene and Juliet Shaman-Burke say in their book *The Mythic Journey: the Meaning of Myth as a Guide for Life*

> There are many myths about marriage; but none describe the 'happy marriage' so many people

> long for. It is, perhaps, ironic that the commonly quoted 'myth' of a happy marriage never appears in mythology. Myth presents us with how things really are psychologically, rather than how we would like them to be. . . . In real life, a happy marriage is the product of human effort and consciousness, and perhaps a bit of good luck as well; but it is not a guaranteed part of the archetypal backdrop of the human psyche. [18]

In her early 40s, at the time of a stressful Neptune aspect Kate remembers feeling an almost desperate longing to be doing more or perhaps to be doing something other than the task at hand. She worked harder and harder until she began to see how she was a workaholic. Kate is the kind of person who likes to plan and strategize about what lies ahead. She anticipates that Neptune's gift in her early 50s could bring her a way to use her professional success to support some kind of charity. Possibly she will get more involved in the arts.

In these times of chaos, we see Neptune in the incredible plethora of panaceas and so-called spiritual teaching applied to everything from achieving enlightenment to buying the right car. One Neptunian lesson we are all familiar with more or less is the fact that if we get conned, in the end, we pay the price for our confusion. Neptune encourages us to dissolve boundaries and become *one with everything.* At the time of Neptune's empowerment we are offered insight into our deepest beliefs; we are pulled toward the song of our soul in subtle yet powerful ways. In a culture that tells us we can satisfy our longings with one more thing, the right relationship, a drug or travel to an exotic destination, it is important to be still and listen. In stillness we can feel the power of longing without feeding it. Neptune's greatest gift is in the ability to do just that. Feeding the longing with more of this or that feels good for a moment but in no way does it lay a foundation for the demands of the inner life that elderhood will bring. By feeling the longing, listening, acknowledging but not acting on it, we remain grounded. When the longing in its intensity passes and we take action in our lives, we are grounded, clear, centered and connected—a truly valuable habit to cultivate.

THE DESCENT TO TRANSFORMATION: PLUTO

Pluto's place in the Greek pantheon is as Lord of the Underworld. For us to understand the meaning of this planet's archetypal symbolism we must include the story of Persephone, Pluto's partner and Queen of the Underworld. Pluto is about the things in this life that call us into descent. In the patriarchal version of Persephone's story she is a hapless maiden, abducted into the underworld by Pluto in one of his rare visits to the upper world. Pluto is invisible above ground. Abduction is easy for him. Given the times in which we live (and who knows how the story was told originally), [19] we might consider that there is another way to conceive this myth. Perhaps there is a strong impulse on the part of the maiden to descend into the underworld.

Once in my early days as an astrologer I was reading a chart for a woman who had a very strong aspect from Pluto. I was telling her the story of Persephone's abduction into the underworld and she stopped me cold. She said I had it all wrong. She *wanted* to explore the dark. Her mother did everything she could to keep her daughter from this kind of descent. From that time on I have revised my interpretation of what Pluto might mean when I tell the story of how Persephone became the queen of the underworld, especially when I tell it to maidens. The following is a new version of the old story, which I hope will be useful to help us see things from a perspective which is relevant to the times in which we live.

This is a story that in ancient times was told and enacted for thousands of years. At the heart of a story like this—a myth—is the power to help us see ourselves. For this power to be manifest down through the ages the story must change to reflect the times in which it is told. This is the wonder of oral traditions: The story changes even as we do. If you are anxious because this telling does not seem true to the form with which you are familiar, remember the old witchy axiom: *She changes everything she touches, everything she touches, changes.*

Once upon a time, a long time ago before houses had been built on this land, when the land looked very different—in a place not too far from here . . .

There lived a mother named Demeter and her daughter Kore. Kore was the light of her mother's life, the joy of her heart. She was wondrous as she grew from infancy through childhood and she spent much of her time in the garden that her mother had created just outside the door to the house. Kore was strong and clever and she loved the plants and animals that she met inside the garden. This garden was very special. The animals sometimes spoke with her and the plants didn't actually talk but somehow Kore knew what each one was used for. Her mother taught her these things before she could remember. It was a happy place—this garden.

On the day that our story begins Kore had come to the end of childhood but was not yet a woman. She was beautiful in the way of all girls on the edge of womanhood. She was still strong and clever but now, she added to her charms the twinkle in her eyes and the almost-smile that played about her mouth.

Demeter was a very protective mother. She made sure that Kore was safe from things that could frighten or damage her. On this day Demeter had to attend to a festival in the fields (it was early spring and she was the Goddess of Grain). She felt that Kore was too old to come with her but not quite old enough to stay home on her own. "Can I just stay home by myself" was often heard in their little house. So Demeter, in her motherly wisdom relented and Kore was allowed to stay home with five young women who were friends as well as handmaidens to the girl.

In this special garden that Demeter had made it seemed as though all the flowers and plants in creation grew. But this was not so. Although Kore didn't know it, there were flowers that she had never seen—Plants that had purposes that she could not yet dream of . . . And there was a boundary around the garden. Before Demeter left she made it very clear that Kore was to stay within the boundary—should she even think about going beyond one of the handmaidens should remind her to stay where it was safe.

And so the afternoon began. At first Kore was content to stay where she had always stayed. Although the territory was familiar to her it was always changing. Every season brought new growth. Things were the same but not the same. As the afternoon wore on Kore—without realizing it—kept moving toward the edge of the garden. Suddenly she looked up and was stunned to see the most beautiful flower. It had beautiful pale yellow petals on the outside but inside was deep orange and it was elegantly balanced on a long green stem. It was taller than most of the flowers that Kore had ever seen. She was filled with an irresistible longing to touch the elegant blossom.

Kore, at this stage in her life was like almost every other girl of her age. She was curious about everything in nature. The flower was the most curious thing she had ever seen. Without realizing what she was doing, Kore moved closer and closer to the flower until she inadvertently walked outside the garden. None of her handmaids noticed that she was outside the garden boundaries because they were too busy admiring the early spring flowers and making flower chains. As Kore was drawn to the flower she had an absolutely uncontrollable urge to pick it. She imagined she would give it to her mother. Perhaps her mother had never seen one like it either!

As Kore plucked the flower an amazing thing happened. The ground under the flower opened up and there before her was a path that seemed to lead down. Kore could not resist. Here was something she had never done, beckoning to her; calling her to step down the path as if it was a dance both ancient and familiar. With barely a glance over her shoulder to see if the maidens had noticed, Kore started off on the downward path thinking she would not go far.

As she walked, the path opened to her and she saw things she had never seen before. Partly this was because she had never been outside at night and the path, as it turned downward and led under the ground, was dark like night. The green things that had so many different shades in the sunlight began to fade into a green so dark it looked black. The songs and sounds of the birds and animals began to change and get quieter. Voices called out to one another with a sound of longing that was never heard during the day. The maiden was truly fascinated.

After walking for who knows how long she eventually came to a place that felt like bottom. Here she found herself at the threshold of a room. At the centre of the room was an old woman dressed in black, with radiant black stones on her fingers and in her ears. Her hair was as white as snow and the gaze that emanated from her black eyes was strong and true. In her right hand she held a long spoon which she stirred into a bubbling cauldron. Without looking up she said, "Good evening, daughter. It is good to see you." The maiden was glad to be welcomed (she had been frightened that something bad might happen to her, but even this fear could not overcome her curiosity). She asked the woman what she was stirring in her cauldron. They began to talk and the old woman—named Hecate—answered the maiden's questions readily. These were questions about things that hadn't seemed to occur to Kore before. They were questions about the dark, about mysteries, long sensed but never articulated. As the maiden and the old crone spoke to one another there entered into the room a man who was Hecate's grandson, Hades. He had never seen a maiden as beautiful as this one (indeed there were not many maidens in this part of the world) and he was instantly smitten with a powerful love as he saw her there, next to his grandmother, conversing so easily. As is the way of things eventually the maiden noticed the young man. She was attracted to the smoky promise in his eyes.

After what seemed like no time at all to the maiden, the old woman, asked gently if her mother, Demeter knew where she was. Kore was struck! It was as if the memory of her mother had faded completely from her mind. Suddenly she was aware that she had gone where she was told not to and had no idea how much time had gone by. She stood up to go and looked around at the old woman, the cauldron, the shelves on the walls stacked with ointments and herbs—she looked out to where Hades stood looking back at her and she asked, "May I return? This is a place I never knew existed, yet it feels like my true place."

Hecate took from the pocket of her robe a pomegranate. She cut it in 3 pieces. One she gave to Hades, one to the maiden and one for herself. Then she said, "If you eat even six of the seeds of this fruit you may come and stay with us for half the year. If we eat of the same fruit, may our destinies be united for all time. But, child, before you eat you must return to the upper world and see for yourself what you leave behind. If you decide to stay with us, even for a little while each year your name will be Persephone."

As the maiden who was Kore and would become Persephone made her way back to the garden of her childhood she began to realize many things. Although it seemed to her that she had been gone no longer than a few hours, for the people above the earth she had been gone for an entire year. Demeter in her deep grief at having lost her daughter was distraught and had ceased to make the crops grow. The garden of Kore's childhood was barren and empty. Humans were hungry and sorrow was everywhere. The other thing that Kore-who-would-be-Persephone realized was that during her time in the underworld she had become a most beautiful woman. Her breasts were full, her belly round, her hair was long and lustrous and her lips red and womanly.

When, finally, she found her mother their joy at being reunited was profound. Demeter too had changed. Grief had etched lines in her face and turned some of her hair to grey. But the love of mother and daughter is stronger than grief and time. They embraced one another and spoke of what had happened while they had been apart.

What we know of that meeting is that Kore chose to eat six of the seeds of her pomegranate—and become Persephone. She realized that she could not fully abandon her life above ground, her mother, and the pure joy of spring. Yet she would go, for six months of every year to Hecate and Hades. There she would learn the mysteries of the dark and become fully alive in both worlds. For her part, Demeter accepted the choice her daughter made because she understood the power of growth and change that always leads to decline and death. No longer would crops grow all year round but for at least six months a year there would be ample time to grow enough food to feed the animals and humans of the earth. The End

Astrological Pluto may be about abduction and being overpowered but it can also be about willing descent and the possibility of seeking and finding the power that lies within.

Pluto represents the power of transformation. One aspect of this is death and where Pluto is concerned death always leads to new life. Winter becomes spring; maidens become mothers and produce more maidens. When Pluto is at work in us we are fascinated, compelled even obsessed with something that we cannot swallow nor can we spit it out. We are often not aware of Pluto's powers at work in our lives in the same way we can't actually see our composted vegetables turning into fertile soil to eventually be put back into the garden.

Pluto is the most alchemical of principles. Its nature is psychological, shamanic and initiatory. All myths and fairy tales where the hero or heroine must descend to transform are stories that come from Pluto's realm. It is not particularly emotional because it is about the inevitability of events. *As you sew, so shall you reap* is a Plutonian motto. Although not emotional in its impulse it can generate powerful emotions in people because it brings up fear of change and loss. As Pluto empowers us it offers profound psychological acceptance. It moves us toward a deeper understanding of what it means to be human as a part of nature rather than apart from it; we are, each and every one of us, capable of so much good and so much ill; we partake of "Nature, red in tooth and claw." [20] This is what is bred in the bone. Pluto is about the inevitability of certain things: If I am born, I will die. If I am born female, I will bleed and not die. These things just are what they are, and in so being they are the greatest mysteries of our lives.

An interesting thing about Pluto is the fact that Pluto has a very elliptical orbit and therefore travels through some signs more quickly than others. For those of us becoming elders in the late 1990s and early twenty-first century Pluto is roughly in sync with Uranus and Neptune. For those born much earlier, Pluto may have done this when you were much older, and for those born much later, Pluto will do this when you are younger than fifty. Given that Pluto's orbit is so erratic, you might find it interesting to check the table at the back of the book to see approximately when Pluto makes the elder aspect to the placement of Pluto when you were born. (See Appendix I: Astrology Tables.)

We might say that Pluto offers us permission to surrender to forces more powerful than we imagine ourselves to be. It is important to remind yourself when considering surrender in the light of Pluto that there is a big difference between surrender and capitulation. If we capitulate we are out of the game. We don't like the way things are, we acknowledge that we can't change it but we withdraw our energy from the process. When we surrender we accept what is regardless of whether it pleases us or not and we stay present to what is happening.

For Esther the effects of Pluto were felt in a particularly difficult interaction with her brother's daughter, her beloved niece. Since she had no children of her own, Esther had a special relationship with this niece. She often doted on the girl's talents and beauty. At the time of Pluto's trine in her early fifties, Esther backed away from the relationship with her brother. At this time the girl began, first subtly and then in a more confrontational way, to side with her father against Esther. One afternoon after a lavish morning of shopping when Esther had essentially purchased the girl a new wardrobe they were having lunch at the Russian Tea Room in New York City. Suddenly out of nowhere her niece began to list all the things that Esther had done which hurt her brother's feelings. It seemed that no detail was missing and perhaps a few had been added. Esther was first stunned, then defensive and finally just plain angry at having been set up in such a way. Try as she might to reason with this young woman in the end she realized that the girl was her father's daughter, and nothing could be done about it. Maybe one day she would see things differently, but all Esther could do was to let go and wait. Nature would have to take its course.

In the process of dealing with this painful situation Esther was reminded of the constant emotional upheavals of her childhood. Her family was only a fragment of a much larger family with many relatives who stayed on in Russia only to vanish in the revolution. Even the ones who came with her grandparents were estranged from one another. For her, the power of the inevitable losses of extended family that happened before she was born made for a lonely and personally difficult childhood with parents who always seemed depressed for no reason she could understand as a child. What she learned at the Pluto trine was that she was not responsible nor could she change the effects of a family broken apart by events larger than any of them. By letting go and accepting things as they are she empowered herself to be present to her life with all the intensity of its joys and sorrows.

Nothing is really secure in Pluto's realm. How could it be if what we are talking about is the inevitable process of life itself? Think of Pluto as the Great Composter. It breaks down the structure of one thing and turns it into another. I'm not sure how it feels to be an onion in a compost heap, but I'm sure that it doesn't argue with the process; it just does what it does until it becomes fertile soil in which another onion can grow. Think of Pluto as who we are in the naked, dark. We do not experience ourselves the same way in the dark of night as we do by the light of day. Pluto symbolically represents the way the past comes to bear on the present and the future. It represents inevitable truths that we might prefer never to bring to consciousness but which are harbored in the depths of our being.

One of the ways you know you are in Pluto's realm is when something happens that brings up a visceral memory of an event from long ago. We would like to think we can leave difficult and troubling experiences from the past behind. Even so, the possibility of being triggered into remembering an event that happened so long ago you can hardly remember it remains until we take our last breath. We might prefer never to bring to consciousness some of the terrible things that have happened to us in the past but these things seem to live in the depths of our being. As we strive to make a solid foundation for our elder years, we must have the courage to face the simple and profound truth which is that a solid foundation does not exist in the material world. All that is created comes to an end. The foundation we are building is within, and in the case of Pluto it is also down under.

When she was in her early fifties, Linda's father died. Her relationship with her father had always been a troubled one, and at the end of his life he remained a difficult and at times unbearable person to spend time with. As he lay dying, Linda rehearsed many possible ways in which her father might show his remorse or sorrow at how much suffering he had caused Linda and the rest of the family. Although as a psychologist she knew better, she found herself obsessing over the possibility of his last words. She bargained with the universe that she would be willing to take heart even if those words were not spoken to her directly. She almost convinced herself that this would happen but her father died as he had lived: frightened, bitter and nasty. After he was gone Linda began to appreciate the terrible yet wonderful initiation that his death offered to her. When you truly love someone it isn't because of who they are, it isn't even in spite of who they are, it's just because they are. You can imagine that in her work with bereaved clients, this was a most valuable lesson from her father.

After the intense emotion of her father's passing subsided, Linda remembered how there had been whispers in her childhood to the effect that her father had been a different person before he went off to war. No one said it outright, but as she put the pieces together after his death, it became clear to her that his war experience must, in fact, have been at the root of his alcoholism and all the ensuing suffering that emerged from it for her and her family.

Because Pluto moves so slowly through the zodiac it is not difficult to know which group you are a part of. The oldest group to be reading this book would have Pluto in Cancer. This generation started at the time of the First World War and ended just after the beginning of the Second World War. (See Appendix I.) Cancer is the sign that symbolizes our connection to the extended family. During this period of two world wars and a depression the family as the cornerstone of society began to experience tremendous upheaval which lives on to the present day. Pluto unearthed family ties through the effects of war and the resulting Diaspora as well as the need for family members to leave home in the Great Depression and find work wherever it might exist. This too resulted in family members living far apart from one another. It began to become more common for children to grow up with only scant connection to grandparents, aunts, uncles and cousins. It is as if the institution of the family went into the compost bin during Pluto's journey through Cancer. As elders, this group must grapple with the knowledge that both their family of origin as well as the one they created as adults were shaped and molded in the times during which they existed. Denial about family matters is a serious impediment to having a truly integrated and loving family.

Pluto was only discovered in 1930. People born after that are the first generation to have Pluto in their charts from their birth along with the astrological possibility of knowing it. Although there have always been people who bring the kind of change that the outer planets represents the energy of these transpersonal planets is said to be available to the general population only after they have been discovered. One of the most powerful events associated by astrologers with the discovery of Pluto is the development of the atom bomb—one of those things that has changed the world forever. Another possibly less dramatic in its appearance but not in its effects on western civilization is the birth of the self-help movement which is said to have begun in 1935 with the establishment of Alcoholics Anonymous. Much of what has filtered down to the general public through self help books and through the media has been distilled as well as adulterated from wisdom that comes to us through the development of depth psychology in the late nineteenth and early twentieth centuries. Pluto is the planet that symbolized depth psychology because one must dive deep into the murky realm of the underworld to find the roots of dis-ease.

The generation of Pluto in Leo was born in the early 1940s through the late 50s. They seem to have the mandate to transform the endlessly confusing quality of self-esteem, which is a Leo issue. Although the bomb was developed when Pluto was in Cancer, it wasn't used until Pluto went into Leo. The generation with Pluto in Leo are constantly drawn to peak experiences. They love the experience of breaking through even if they must blast through. This is the generation of the baby boomers. Everyone is part of a generation; you have no choice in this matter. You can either attempt to remove yourself from it in your own mind or identify with it, but you will somehow be in relationship to it. It is interesting to contemplate how being part of such a constantly lauded and criticized group may have affected your life. As elders this generation needs to let go of their image of who they are and instead accept themselves as they *actually* are—warts and all. This was a generation that didn't believe they would ever grow old. For this generation, Pluto's challenge in becoming an elder requires a process of finding the true self apart from the image of the self. They must learn to embrace the authenticity of who they are in a way that can only be evaluated subjectively to see if it holds truth.

The youngest group to use this book will be those with Pluto in Virgo born in the very late 1950s through the beginning of the 1970s. This is the group born in a time when the nuts and bolts of our lives were changing rapidly. They grew up with junk food and TV. The sixties have gone down in history as a time of great cultural change and disorientation. This group struggles to find their transformation through their work, their health and the health of the planet. As elders they will be in a position to mentor those younger to help bring the world to its senses regarding how we treat the earth and each other. They are meant to be healers of the Earth in their elder wisdom. The more they surrender to the natural cycles of life, the easier this will be.

As she anticipates this transition in her life Kate is well aware of the value she places on work. In her 40s she was forced to transition from employee to consultant. At the time she was angry and humiliated that her company was letting her go. Although her distress was great she has become quite successful in running her own consulting business. Looking back she is glad that she made the change even if it wasn't her choice at the time. Looking ahead Kate considers what it would be like to take a partner into her business as she gets older. This would allow her to put more energy into charity work but it would also entail giving up some control. She feels comforted by the fact that she can think ahead and consider who she might be interested in and how the details of sharing her little empire might work.

For exercises that pertain to working with the symbolism of Pluto in your chart, go to Appendix II: Exercises: Pluto.

Overall, this period from age forty-nine to fifty-five offers a significant moment in a person's life, in which it's possible to glimpse the powerful forces that swirl around and within us all the time. This is not a time of good luck or ease but rather a time when we are asked to acknowledge without qualifiers who we are—not who we wish we were or who we might have been—no ifs, ands, or buts. On a personal level you may face tough circumstances. Any number of difficulties can beset us at any age. Even so, through it all, we are developing the ability to hold to an underlying acceptance of the fact that this *is* life. This simple, profound understanding can empower us if we let it.

Even for those who lack the desire to grow in awareness, this period offers a kind of strength as well. The sense of empowerment that comes from just being who you are filters through. Although this may feel good at the time, without the awareness that it won't last—that you will change as time passes—you may feel strong, but this strength will not sustain itself unless you are aware of the wisdom that can grow from it: Change is inevitable and surrender to change is profoundly empowering on an inner level. This might be a time when you feel at the top of your game, or perhaps you just feel the need to be at the top. It may also be a time when you are overwhelmed by more personal and seemingly demanding issues, yet you stand firm in dealing with them. After all, everyone, including yourself, expects that you know how to handle most situations by now. However you look at it, it seems that whether or not you feel accomplished there is a way in which people at this stage of life—from forty-nine through fifty-four—have the ability to observe themselves being themselves in a unique way. Whether you know it or not, you have come to the high point of your adult life and will soon be crossing the line into your elderhood.

No matter what your chronological age is as you read this book, if you are over fifty-five you have passed through this powerful stage. Whether you created a solid foundation at that time or not, you can always pay attention to these glimpses of your true self: your ideals, your deeply held beliefs, the psychological complexes that run your life, and how you do and don't get your needs met. Be present to what you see, and you will have an excellent foundation for the next stage in the unfolding journey of becoming an elder in times of chaos.

Chapter 3

Holy Sparks

In your mid-fifties, you may have a strong sense of who you are and what is expected of you. You have learned that experience is the best teacher, and you have been called to apply the wisdom you have gained from your experience to more than one situation. You might even have developed a sense that life is something you can or must accept. Some challenges to the stability that we create in our early fifties seem to begin at around fifty-five or fifty-six. If your foundation is solid, then as the territory gets more demanding you will be prepared.

The way that astrologers generally refer to the period that begins around fifty-six is as the Saturn Return. But as we shall see there are many other things that occur in this period of the second half of the fifties. We will work with the astrological principles of Saturn as well as the Ascendant, the Sun, Jupiter, the Moon, the nodes and Uranus (once again). Another way of saying this is that we will explore our relationship as elders to the principles of responsibility, persona, our heart's desire, fundamental beliefs, temperament, karma and the need for freedom.

As you unfold the symbolic information that each of these holds, try not to focus too much on the exact moment at which things happen but to understand that it is all part of the continuum of the experience of becoming an elder. At any time, as you make the transition from adult to elder, any one of these things can arise as worthy of your consideration. After you have crossed into the realm of the elders, reflection on these themes will remain valuable for years to come. When we think symbolically as we do with astrology, time is not necessarily linear. The past and the future are more fluid than we think and can arise in our mind and emotions when we least expect it. If you are present enough in your awareness to recognize when this happens you can be sure it will help you grow in wisdom. At seventy you may recollect an experience that happened when you were fifty-nine. By reflecting on how it made you feel, and how it still makes you feel, you can reorient yourself to the meaning of this experience. This quality of reflection becomes more important as we age. As Jungian analyst Helen Luke put it:

> You know that as we grow older we start remembering old things much more clearly than what happened yesterday. In fact one has trouble remembering yesterday. It can just be nostalgia, without meaning, and it often is. Or it can be a rediscovery of the whole pattern of your life as a circle or a spiral . . . The spiral goes into the dark, into the light, into the dark, into the light. It goes up or down. It goes around. It is the image of the life of the spiritual in humans. [1]

Esther is our oldest elder. She became sixty in 1996. On 9/11 she, like millions of others, lived in New York City. As the horror of what happened and was still to happen took hold in her psyche she felt at a loss to integrate it into her understanding of the world. While reviewing the past year in January 2002, she reread a section on her fundamental belief system in the journal she had kept during an elder workshop in Toronto. Out of the blue I received a phone call thanking me for making her aware of the fact that she even had a fundamental world view. The notion of belonging to a specific religion was long abandoned in the journey of her life. By reflecting on the observations she had made regarding this aspect of her life she was able to continue the dialogue with her inner, wise old woman and integrate to some extent her place as an elder in the post 9/11 world. To say she suddenly became radicalized would be an exaggeration, but she wrote letters to newspapers and politicians, joined marches, and helped younger people to move beyond the shock of the attack on their city. If there is one thing we know by the time we are elders it is that we have finally entered the realm where we are *old enough to be wise*. Having a map of the territory can only help.

If you aren't deep in denial, somewhere in your mid-fifties you'll come to the realization that you will have to accept wholeheartedly the incredible changes in your life. In the extremely extroverted culture of the late twentieth and early twenty-first centuries one of the most common perspectives seems to be that this is a time to devote oneself to exercise, health, and fun because all of these things help us to feel young. Some join the gym, others go trekking in interesting and unusual parts of the world. As the economy becomes more and more unstable, many of our expectations about how we will spend our time and money as elders are rapidly changing. None of these choices are inherently bad or good but in truth none of these things really help us to grapple with the underlying issue that presents itself like an uninvited guest at this time. You are heading, one way or another, inevitably closer to your death. Maudlin fascination or desperate fears don't make this concept easier to grapple with. Denial is like a band-aid that buys us time in the moment but doesn't seem to do the trick in the middle of the night or when we find ourselves at the funeral of a parent or friend. Somehow we need to grapple with this powerful, simple, irrevocable truth—that we are getting older and therefore closer to death—without losing our sense of being alive. In reality there is nothing in the world that increases our sense of aliveness better than a healthy perspective on the inevitability of death. I have heard that there are yogis who meditate in charnel grounds. To sit still, surrounded by death, is definitely a way to awaken consciousness!

As elders we have the opportunity to hold the awareness of how ephemeral life is along with our awareness of past generations (what it was like for our parents and grandparents) and future generations (how it will be for the children and their children's children). Accepting the reality of death in the midst of life is to accept death as the natural end of life. What does it mean to have lived at all? What traces do we leave behind after we die? Why does life matter at all? Underlying each of the symbols we will explore from this point on grapples with the question of what it means to have a life and leave it.

Shortly after my fifty-sixth birthday I found this in *God Is a Verb* by Rabbi David A. Cooper:

> The Kabbalah teaches that each year in a person's life, a particular quality is accentuated. The fifty-sixth year of one's life is a period in which one is immersed in the loving side of one's strength, a domain of enormous forgiveness in the cosmic flow and a fresh opportunity to raise holy sparks within and around oneself to higher levels of awareness. [2]

This quote feels to me like an invitation into the second half of our fifties. It suggests how one might deepen their experience of becoming and ultimately being an elder. Up till now we have been laying groundwork; getting used to the idea that we are in our fifties. Our adult head is in the birth canal. The contractions are about immersing ourselves in what Rabbi Cooper calls the "loving side of our strength." This may or may not be your experience at exactly fifty-six but any time you become aware of this it serves as a herald, reminding you that something different is required as we become elders. Once you turn the corner of fifty-five the knowledge begins to dawn that, one way or another, the broadest sense of forgiveness will be required if we are to find any peace as we get older. We may or may not be ready to forgive at the exact moment of our fifty-fifth birthday but as we realize the inevitability of this state we also become aware of the light that radiates out from it as something we might like to experience as we grow older. If not now, when? If I cannot forgive, who then can I expect to forgive me?

I believe what Rabbi Cooper means by "a domain of enormous forgiveness in the cosmic flow" is the awesome realization that this is it. Life is terminal. And we must forgive *life itself* for creating us, knowing all the while that we will have to give it up. This awareness comes in waves, and it spreads out through the rest of your life.

From this enormous forgiveness, which often arrives in moments when we least expect it, comes the "holy sparks." The image of holy sparks comes from Kabbalistic thinking, which says that the soul is attracted to the sparks of holiness that are buried in the physical world. Each of us is born with the potential to recognize these sparks and thereby to make the world whole again. Forgiveness is a powerful way to redeem the holy sparks of our existence.

In the process of forgiving life itself no doubt a person must grapple with all the people (including oneself) that seem to have wronged you in your life. This includes parents, spouses, ex-spouses, children, work colleagues and coworkers, clergy, teachers and so forth. The process of forgiving each and every person who ever hurt or disappointed you is necessary if you want to be free. If you follow the thread like a constellation of stars in a dark night you will eventually come to the need for the Big Forgiveness. You have to forgive life itself for never completely measuring up to all that it could have been. On a good day we may focus on how amazing and generous life has been to us but always, on a bad day we can find the disappointment, the regret, the nagging incredulity that somehow life let us down. Accepting this from time to time as a given is very liberating. The very nature of human existence is fraught with imperfection and disappointment.

Sometimes in a person's life it becomes impossible to forgive those that have hurt us because the hurt is impossible to integrate and there has been no apology or contrition on the part of the perpetrator. These are traumatic issues that live deeply in the body and mind of a person. Although it is not in the scope of this book to suggest a sure-fire way to heal trauma Judith Herman, MD a pioneer in the study of Post-Traumatic Stress Disorder and the sexual abuse of women and children offers us the notion that what is truly required is 'restorative love'.

> Like revenge, the fantasy of forgiveness often becomes a cruel torture because it remains out of reach for most ordinary human beings. Folk wisdom recognizes that to forgive is divine. And even divine forgiveness in most religious systems, is not unconditional. True forgiveness cannot be granted until the perpetrator has sought and earned it through confession, repentance and restitution.
>
> Genuine contrition in a perpetrator is a rare miracle. Fortunately, the survivor does not need to wait for it. Her healing depends on the discovery of restorative love in her own life; it does not require that love be extended to the perpetrator. [3]

One of the more difficult aspects of forgiveness might be that as we lay to rest the sorrow of our personal wrongs we open the door to the terrible things that the world can do to people. We are bombarded with images and information of terrible things in the news of the world as well as in the art that we create, particularly movies and books. Forgiving your mother is easy next to forgiving life or God or however you see it for creating such an imperfect system that allows children to starve and terrorism to flourish at so many levels. As elders we are meant to be able to hold this awareness without denial and with an open heart—for our own good and for the good of all. If we can do that, surely holy sparks will fly! (For an exercise pertaining to forgiveness and/or restorative love, see Appendix II: Chapter 3: Forgiveness and restorative love.)

If you are a baby boomer you probably have a strong sense of *my generation.* [4] As we approach elderhood it is worthwhile to consider how we have been shaped and molded by membership in our generation—no matter what it is. Other people, who also grow old, may want to read and use this book as well. It is not specifically a book for baby boomers. Everyone is part of a generation. Everyone can consider the effect this has had in making them who they are.

My sense of the generations is based on what astrology tells me about them. Assuming that at the most there will be three generations of people who might use this book, I will speak to those three generations. Some of this revisits concepts from Chapter 2 but from a different perspective.

The first group of elders includes those born with Pluto in Cancer and Neptune in Virgo. (See Appendix I for exact dates.) You know who you are if you were born between two world wars and lived through the Great Depression. In a broad and general way you learned to put up with things. Your parents expected their children to be seen but not heard. Your children demanded center stage as well given that the world was fascinated by how many children were being born and what could be done with such a demographic. As a child and as a mother you were expected to take a back seat. Your group is a silent but powerful generation. Often you are surprised at the influence you have had on other people. Your elder years occur at a time when the culture around you is unraveling [5] but still more or less recognizable. If you are lucky enough to benefit from all the life-extending options of the modern world, it is quite possible that you will live on well into the chaos. It never hurts to be prepared!

This is Esther's generation. She grew up at a time when it felt as though her parents had total control over everything she did. For example although she loved to play the piano it felt that she was taking the lessons because her mother demanded it. In a sense she was always playing for her mother.

The second group includes those born with Pluto in Leo and Neptune in Libra. You know yourself if the term "the sixties" means something quite personal to you. You were born at a time when everyone was trying to get back to life as it *should* be, even as the war in Vietnam raged and some adults were locking unruly children in psychiatric hospitals or arresting and shooting at them for protesting. You grew up at a time when there was money to burn and everything could be for sale sooner or later. You were part of (one way or another) what is often termed the sexual revolution. You expected that you could do it better than your parents, no matter what it was. This generation has had some mighty issues around authority. They expect that they are the best and most interesting people that ever lived. They aren't quite so clear about how insecure they are despite their endless appetite for self-improvement. Oprah belongs to this generation. As parents, this group wants their children to like them. They want desperately to be loved and to express their creativity, to be recognized for how great they are. They are becoming elders at a time when the culture around them is quite chaotic. Many of the institutions that were supposed to support them in old age are crumbling, and they can't count on family to support them. Perhaps it will fall to them to reinvent the notion of elder in such a way that it will inspire those younger to make the world a place in which everyone can live.

This is Linda's generation. She has said more than once she felt she was part of a generation of orphans. It seemed that her parents didn't have a clue about what their children needed. On account of this she became a child of the culture and learned about herself more through her peers than from her parents.

The third group that may one day find this process worth exploring have Pluto in Virgo and Neptune in Scorpio. This group is very concerned with their health and their jobs. They are high strung and often want to transform the world through their own individual effort. They believe it is possible to do things efficiently but they often overextend themselves. As they become fully adult the sixty-plus-hour work week, minus benefits, returned. They can dream big dreams but only if they have some kind of realistic vehicle through which to actualize them. Many in this group have taken the sexual revolution to the next level by experimenting with the deeper darker side of intimacy. They were the first to be "out" about just about everything. In their elder years the world may still be in a fair amount of chaos. They will be expected to work long into their old age and that will be fine with them as long as they are healthy enough to pull it off. I suspect that this group spends a lot of time researching the best way to live in all aspects of life. As parents they tend to worry about their children even as they schedule them into their busy work day.

This is Kate's generation. Her reaction to the dark and wild energy of her group was to focus on what she, as an individual, could accomplish so she wouldn't be swept away into the seemingly random energies of the times. Her solution was personal excellence and control over her circumstances in all cases.

If you think about it you will see that the second group was born when the first group was becoming adult and therefore largely parenting the second. The third group was born when the second was doing the same. As the trend for women to have children later and later in their lives becomes more widespread, it can actually occur that you skip a generation. The line between grandparent and parent has blurred as more and more people with distinctly gray hair have young children.

Becoming an elder in times of chaos will have its pros and cons. Much of your experience will depend on your perspective. Out of chaos comes new growth but it's quite likely we will not be here to see it. Our old age will be spent in chaos. I have been pondering this notion for some years in light of the fact that old people don't like change. Maybe because there is such an onslaught of change inside the body-mind as we grow old, we would like the external world to stay predictable. But it does seem, in these times of global warming, escalating terrorism and a wobbly, unpredictable world financial picture that the task that will fall to us will be to grow old amidst chaos. It is up to us to decide if we have been cursed or blessed to live in interesting times. (For an exercise pertaining to your generation, see Appendix II: Chapter 3: Your Generation.)

THE PERSONA

Astrologically speaking we look for the persona in the Ascendant or rising sign; literally the sign which is rising in the east at the moment we take our first breath. This part of your astrological chart indicates how you give birth to and defend yourself.

If we see the transition from adult to elder as real, then we can also think of it as a kind of birth. As well as this being a personal birth into a new stage of life I believe that culturally we are also engaged in giving birth to the notion of an elder as different from an adult. Along with this new awareness (that does, it seems, stem from so many baby boomers approaching their elder years) there is a growing realization that we don't want to do it the way our parents did, and even if we did, our world is not the same as the world they inhabited as elders. Things have definitely changed. Not only is there a developing notion of the elder years, but along with that is the change in the way this period of life is perceived by non-elders. If nothing else the baby boomers are (and have always been) an incredible market for whatever stage of life they are going through. Our parents moved into this stage of life with the concept of retirement. For men it might have been about the gold watch and the package that could come with retirement, for women perhaps more about supporting retirement. Women didn't generally get the gold watch but many enjoyed being grandparents and perhaps their extended family. They thought this was their time to do the things they'd always wanted to do with or without their partners.

All births involve death. The thing that you were must give way to the thing that you are becoming. Transformation is a funny kind of word. People like the sound of it but in reality it means to change the form of something. That is never easy. The first time we tried it was when we left our mother's womb. Most of us don't remember that moment but it is indelibly etched into our consciousness. Astrologically it shows up loud and clear in the Ascendant.

The Ascendant or Rising Sign is an important part of the astrological picture. It is calculated by taking the moment of a person's first breath at the longitude and latitude of the place where they took that breath. Simply put, it is the sign that is rising in the east at the moment when you first experience yourself as separate. Anything that happens in the east astrologically represents birth because this is where the Sun is "born" every morning as it rises. This is a moment fraught with the instinct to survive after having come through the dangerous and difficult experience of birth.

The astrological Ascendant describes the personality of an individual. Psychologically speaking we could say that the first moment of life experienced outside the womb provides the raw material out of which we create our persona. While we are in the womb we are alive but not separate. We take in all sorts of information but we have no opinion about it. The actual experience of having been born changes all that. I believe what actually happens is that our perspective about who we are begins to take shape according to the experience we have that enabled us to accomplish such a feat as birth. The quality of this perspective can be seen in the Ascendant. This then becomes the reference point for the identity that we will ultimately see as our "self." The human mind seems to work through analogy. The way we learn new things is to compare and contrast them with things we already know. The birth experience provides the fundamental material to which we compare everything that follows. Astrologically we see this in the Ascendant but, as always, even if you don't actually know your Ascendant, you can think with great personal insight about your personality which is essentially the same thing.

If you aren't sure what time you were born, you will find a simple keyword description of the twelve possibilities in the keyword appendix for this chapter. (Appendix I: Signs) Simply turn to the keywords and choose the description that seems to fit. As long as it fits, use it. If at some point in your exploration another sign seems to express these things better, try that one on. Although this seems imprecise, it is fine to try one on and see how it makes you feel. You will definitely learn something about yourself even if in the end you decide it isn't the right one! Whether or not you know what to call it astrologically, you have a personality that identifies you and you know more or less how it functions.

The Ascendant is the first assumption we made about what life is like. We held on to it with all our might because it was the only thing with which we could identify. By holding on tightly to this basic assumption, this first cause, we survived. Survival is always something to be respected. The Ascendant or persona is a powerful statement about an individual because it is associated with all that survival requires.

One of the most difficult things about the persona or Ascendant is that it is always laced with a kind of fear or defensiveness. We use it to remind ourselves that we are separate and that we can literally live with that separateness. Without it we wouldn't be able to know who we are. It forms the cornerstone for the personality. Long after we need to be worried about immediate survival we still use the Ascendant as the lens through which we see the world. It is also the way people who know us personally see us.

One thing that happens as we become elders is that we come to a point again and again where we see that our persona has too much power over us. It isn't something that we see once and then change. It ambushes us over and over again. This process of realizing that the habitual responses of your personality may not be the way you really want to act begins in your 40s. That is the last gasp of making the persona into what you want it to be. In our fifties we are trying to find a way of comfortably being ourselves. Although our persona may be habitual and familiar it isn't the whole picture of who we are. You could think of your persona metaphorically as a car that you drive in a land of no pedestrian walkways. It enables you to get around. Even if you lose it in the parking lot, it's easy to identify because it has a license plate. But it's the driver inside that makes it go. Taking care of your vehicle is important and, truth to tell, sooner or later it does start showing signs of age. Despite the importance of having a means to get around, most people are pretty clear that they are more than their vehicle. Cultivating the awareness that there is more to you than meets the eye allows you to be confident in knowing that who you seem to be isn't the entirety of who you are.

This would be easier if the Ascendant wasn't laced with a survival instinct that tries to defend and protect you from anything that threatens its existence! The Ascendant or persona gives us the illusion that we know the territory. If the territory is inherently unknown and constantly changing (as is the way of becoming and being an elder) it is not useful to take a defensive stance. In this sense, the Ascendant keeps us from being present. The persona is a tricky character because it endlessly tries to convince us that we are threatened. Fear and defensiveness strengthen its position.

And yet we need it. It is the body in which we live. It is literally the way we can recognize ourselves when we wake up in the morning and it is the way others recognize us. The trick is to use it, to wear it so to say, but not to identify with it. (If you would like to do an Ascendant exercise go to Appendix II: Exercises: Ascendant)

For Esther working with the information about her Ascendant confirmed for her the endless need she had to get her family to accept her the way she is as part of the group. She can see that part of the problem was the lack of extended family. There were not aunts and uncles whom she might have been more like and who could have validated her way of being. The feeling of never truly bonding with a family group has motivated much of her behavior throughout her life.

Working with the information she gathered from studying her Ascendant, Linda realized without too much surprise that her intellectual prowess and her ability to wield the sword of truth, although often brilliant, was the way she defended herself against the outrage she felt at the injustices that went on in her family of origin. She could not defend the family against her father's behavior but she could explain it to them. Most of all she could explain it to herself. The good thing about this is that it enabled her to get a good education. The drawback is that she can have a hard time knowing what she really feels.

Kate sees her workaholic tendencies through her Ascendant. Working with this information she has become aware that her striving was a reaction against the chaos that seemed to rage outside the home, in the larger culture. She had a sense that even her parents could not hold back the random possibilities of the world. She worked hard to achieve mastery in such a way that she might be prepared to manage any situation that might arise for her or her loved ones.

We are challenged as elders to be the person we have been conditioned to be without identifying with it as if it is all we are.

One of the most basic ways that this comes home to us is in the fact that the Ascendant is the body. It is how we look as well as how we see into the world. As it gets older and develops its little weaknesses or big ones we are forced to break the identification. It's all practice for the ultimate breaking of identification when we leave the body all together.

If we believe that there is a difference between our adult and elder selves, that we do indeed cross a threshold at this time of life, then we must practice breaking our identification without losing our identity. Whenever we let go of identification with something familiar we inevitably experience the insecurity of not knowing who we are or what's next. Although this can be unsettling it is the best time to learn new things about ourselves and the world.

Due to the inherent difficulty of needing our identity even as we need to become less attached to it, one could say there is a particular kind of suffering that goes with this process. You can hold onto identification with the ego and suffer because you stop growing or you can break the identification and suffer because you feel awfully insecure when you can't follow your old habits to protect yourself. In *Old Age,* Helen M. Luke says: "The roots of all our neuroses lie here, in the conflict between the longing for growth and freedom and our incapacity or refusal to pay the price in suffering of the kind which challenges the supremacy of the ego's demands. . . . The ego will endure the worst agonies of neurotic misery rather than one moment of consent to the death of even a small part of its demand or its sense of importance." [6]

Another way of looking at this is to consider that, although you are an expert in being yourself, if you want to learn anything new you will have to give up having the answer and allow yourself to ask the question. As the great Zen master Shunryu Suzuki once said: "In the beginner's mind there are many possibilities, but in the expert's there are few." (7)

(For an exercise pertaining to the Ascendant or rising sign, see Appendix II: Chapter 3: Your Ascendant or rising sign.)

Chapter 4

Faith and the Heart's Desire

The Sun is the fire at the heart of the solar system. Remote as it is from us in distance, it warms us and creates environments in which countless organisms go through the cycle of life on earth. Symbolically we say that the Sun in a person's astrological chart represents their heart's desire. Most if not all of the people reading this book know their Sun sign. This is the sign the Sun was in on the day you were born. Appendix I discusses the subject of cusps.

Jupiter is a companion to the Sun. The Sun lights up the solar system. It is a star, our star. Jupiter is almost big and gaseous enough to be a Sun in its own right but luckily not quite. Still, it is the biggest planet in the solar system and even if it is mostly hot air it has a lot to tell us. Symbolically Jupiter represents our basic assumptions about what is good and bad and/or right and wrong.

Astrologically speaking the Sun and Jupiter represent our relationship to the father principle. Speaking from an archetypal perspective it is the mother's place to bring us into this life, to nourish and sustain us in infancy and through childhood and to teach us the ins and outs of the practical world such as: The iron is **hot.** The road is **dangerous**. It is the other parent's or father's role to help us to move out from that safe place. The parent in the father role (be it he or she) is there to help us navigate our moral and creative behavior. Our father is meant to encourage us to take risks and to understand what is right and wrong. Our mother is meant to love us no matter what we do. She tends more toward the unconditional side of love. My point here isn't about gender. In recent times we have seen many more men taking the role of nurturing parent as well as mothers going out into the world and thereby becoming the 'other' parent. My point here is that the Sun and Jupiter symbolize energies that are meant to take us out into the world, away from the safe place. To do that in a nuclear family, we need a second parent.

In extended families a child is encouraged out into the world by a variety of people. Aunts and Uncles as well as fathers are equally right for the task. The extended family often has existed within a larger framework of strict gender role definitions. It then would be common that the boys go out into the world under the guidance of the men. Women are prepared for marriage—the assumption being that they will leave their birth family and enter their husband's family. As family structure becomes more nuclear, two parents plus children, the role of the father is dominated by a single person.

A possibly optimistic spin on the breakdown of the nuclear family over the second half of the 20th century is that it has inadvertently led to many children growing up with more than one set of parents and relatives. In its own strange way this period in history might be the early days of a society which is made up of more extended types of family without rigid gender stereotypes.

Keep in mind as you read on that even as you delve into your identity as the daughter of your father or the partner of the father of your children you are also exploring your relationship to your own heart's desire (Sun) and your basic assumptions (Jupiter) about life. The connection between the father figures and the inner realm lies in the fact that these aspects of yourself were most likely conditioned by the behavior of your father, uncles or even the fathers of your friends. In actuality we know that there are many single parents, fathers who offer a safe haven and mothers who encourage their children to take risks whether or not it might be comfortable for them. Inasmuch as we were children once and perhaps we have been parents, it is good to know that there is room for all combinations as we engage these symbolic pictures.

In the chaotic world of the early twenty-first century global village the father principle is severely damaged. We can see this in the deadbeat dads as well as the widespread ineptitude and even corruption of men in power. Courage and morality (qualities connected with the Sun and Jupiter, respectively) have too often been twisted into the opposite qualities of cowardice, dogmatic fundamentalism and unethical behavior. For at least the last 5000 years we have been participating in an experiment of domination: Men over women, humans over nature, rich over poor, white over black. I believe that this culture of domination has seriously damaged the symbolic integrity of the Sun and Jupiter. As archetypal principles they represent a pure form of energy. Each age has a way of translating the essential quality of an archetype by filtering it through the prevailing metaphors of the day. If dominance is the prevailing metaphor then the Sun (our hearts desire) and Jupiter (our core beliefs) are twisted through that lens.

The Sun represents the king. A truly noble king is the servant of the people; all the people. A good king is not a power hungry dominator of the people. The power accorded a ruler is sacred and should never be used for personal gain or manipulation. When this happens tyranny will eventually be the result. As you may have noticed there has rarely been a person in power in this world for many centuries who is not motivated by the urge to dominate rather than to serve. Jupiter represents the advisor, the wise judge. This principle also has been bent through the lens of domination. It has come to represent those who manipulate us into war along with the belief that we have the righteous imperative to kill those who don't agree with us. We have come to a time in the world when these principles must find the noble side of their expression or all could be lost.

It would appear that we live in an age of the wounded king. It is possible however that despite the moral disorder of these times the very existence of the wounded king calls out the need for healing in many individuals. We see this whenever someone is fearless in their ability to do the right thing for others without power agendas.

To understand more about the wounded king we can turn to the Arthurian Legends and the myth of Parzival. The way the story goes in short form is that Parzival is a knight raised in a dark wood by only his mother. She is so distraught about the dangers of the life of a knight that she wants to protect her precious son from the knowledge that this is his inheritance. Parzival grows into early adolescence not even knowing the word for knight. Needless to say one day a knight comes riding, flashing armor, wielding weapons and sitting astride a majestic steed. Parzival is struck at once and thinks he is seeing an angel. In no time he forsakes his mother and rides off into the world with the knight. Early on in his travels he comes to the Grail Castle, which has become a wasteland because the king is sick (he is wounded in the groin). Parzival meets the sick king as well as the Grail Maiden, more beautiful than all imagining. Something is expected of Parzival in this moment but although he is pure as can be he is too inexperienced to ask the right question. He has been taught and follows the rules of the society and not the dictates of his own heart. On account of this he cannot find the right question to ask and in an instant castle, king and maiden disappear. Many years later after much experience, suffering and some hard-won wisdom—the kind that can only come from experience—Parzival comes once again to the castle. This time he knows which questions to ask. The king is healed, as is the wasteland of the heart, the fatherless desert. Now it becomes a fertile and life-giving realm once again. [1]

As a culture we are still waiting for the Wasteland to be restored. As W.B. Yeats so eloquently put at the beginning of the twentieth century in his poem *The Second Coming*: "Things fall apart; the center cannot hold; Mere anarchy is loosed upon the world" . . . The best lack conviction, while the worst are full of passionate intensity." [2] Perhaps it is the job of the elders, as we explore the realm of the heart, to figure out and ask the right questions.

Fathers everywhere have lost the respect of their children and with this also can be the loss of a sense of purpose and integrity about one's own life. As sons are estranged from their fathers they also lose knowledge of what is expected of them as fathers. This contributes significantly to chaos. Out of such chaos will undoubtedly emerge a new and more appropriate father archetype than the one which has taken shape in our culture of domination. Perhaps, if we are lucky, the new father will respect the mother as well as his own valuable contribution to parenting his children. Perhaps these chaotic times can be seen as a period of transition with the possibility of new patterns emerging to replace the ways of domination.

Our issue here isn't to lament the perceived weakness and ineffectiveness of fathers but to acknowledge our own place as elders in the chaotic and unpredictable season of no one in charge. Especially when ethics are questionable all around and there is a serious dearth of courage. As women in the elder stage of our lives we become freer from the biologically imposed tasks of women. It is appropriate for us to feel called to fill in this gap; to stand for what we believe in and to help society to create new models for moral and ethical behavior.

THE HEART OF THE MATTER: THE SUN

Just about everyone knows his or her Sun sign. When someone asks you, "What's your sign?" and you tell them, "Leo" or "Capricorn" what they are really asking is, "What sign was the Sun in when you were born?" When you tell them you are telling them what time of year you were born. The way we determine the signs is through the seasons as they are known to us in the northern hemisphere. [3]

The Sun is the brightest thing in the sky. It lights up the day. Literally and symbolically there is nothing more powerful. It represents our strongest personal connection to spirit. It is the clear light of day which allows us to see the world as it is; the light that illuminates the darkness; the light at the end of the tunnel. When you get to the end of the road, the end of the journey, the end of your life the Sun is the thing you want to know you accomplished.

If you have ever wondered why Sun sign astrology is so popular perhaps the reason lies in the fact that the Sun represents the heart of a person; the thing about which they would like to be most proud. Because of this we can be both flattered and insulted by the story it tells. People don't really read their daily horoscope because it will tell them how to live their lives but because they may find a clue to what is in their own hearts. The Scorpio finds comfort or at least validation in the description that says she is intense as does the Capricorn in the message that she is a natural manager. It is like finding a clue in the sand that might help you solve the mystery of what you would most like to achieve in this life as well as how to achieve it.

The astrological Sun has a very different feeling than the Ascendant which we discussed in the previous chapter. The Ascendant defends, defines and protects us, the Sun is that which we strive to become.

By the time we are on the road to becoming elders it is clear that over-identification with our persona or Ascendant can hold us back from achieving what calls to us from our heart or Sun. One of the key notions I use to differentiate the personality and the authentic heart's desire (Ascendant and Sun) is the notion of false and true pride. False pride occurs when we have to hold something up for the sake of how it looks or how we want others to see us. True pride is nothing less than self-esteem, a necessary quality if we want to live out our heart's desire.

If we have not done so already there is no better time than our elder years to finally lay claim to an authentic sense of self-esteem. The most powerful factor leading up to healthy self-esteem is self-acceptance. At this period of our lives we may come to realize that we have lived long enough, and experienced enough defensive behavior to last us the rest of our lives. What we are ready to do is finally, actually and simply believe in ourselves.

Esther who has the Sun in Leo finds it a true self-esteem booster that she can live her life and support herself by doing what she values most—teaching people to express themselves through their bodies. Linda, a Taurus is equally proud of her ability to do the thing she values most; to help others transform their lives. She is especially proud to have transformed her own life to such a degree that she can use the wisdom she has gained to aid others. Kate who has the Sun in Scorpio has a long-standing tradition of believing in herself based on her successes in both her personal and professional life. Although she is aware that she has been very fortunate in many external ways such as having been born to her parents and given so many opportunities, her self-esteem most often comes from a feeling of inward self-mastery of her desires and impulses that allows her to be in control of her responsibilities.

(For an exercise pertaining to the Sun in your own horoscope go to: Appendix II: Chapter 4: The Sun)

OUR VISION OF TRUTH: JUPITER

Now that we have looked at the Sun we are ready to explore the symbolic message of Jupiter. In the Greek pantheon of gods and goddesses Zeus is the father of the gods. We know him astrologically by his Roman name, Jupiter. His thunderbolt decides who is right and who is wrong. He is the ultimate judge. Perhaps some of Jupiter's qualities can be intuited from its actual behavior in our solar system. For example, "'Jupiter's gravity has helped protect Earth from being hit by comets.'" [4] As a symbol of truly righteous wisdom Jupiter's meaning in our chart is meant to indicate ways in which we can protect ourselves from injustice and ignorance. At the time when we actually cross over the threshold from adult to elder we have a Jupiter return. Jupiter returns to its natal position in your chart about every twelve years. The return at 60 is considered more significant than most because only at 60 does it return so close to Saturn's return which only happens every 29-30 years (see Chapter 6). When you are somewhere between the ages of 58-60 both Jupiter and Saturn are in the position they held at your birth.

Chinese astrology is based on a twelve year cycle in which each year is represented by an animal. It is not tied to the constellations as is western astrology but was originally linked to the cycle of Jupiter. Although the Chinese system of astrology seems very different it is just another perspective drawing on the same information. Certainly it confirms the universal significance of the Jupiter cycle. The ultimate cycle in the Chinese system is 60 years (five twelve year cycles) which coincides with the cycle of the Saturn/Jupiter return in an individual's chart. In the branch of Western astrology called mundane or political astrology, this conjunction is considered highly significant. It is thought to symbolize the coming together for good or ill of law (Jupiter) and order (Saturn).

Symbolically Jupiter is associated with learning, teaching, vision and philosophy. It tells us about our belief systems, the fundamental belief systems that inform our philosophy, religion and even our every day moral choices. Jupiter is about what religion we practice, if we practice, and what religion we might have been raised in. All religions of the world try to teach us how to live. In today's world there is a division between secular and religious culture. Many people do not practice a specific religion. Nonetheless everyone has a belief system that helps them decide what is moral and what is not. Astrologically we equate this universal component of the human experience with Jupiter. Even if you don't call yourself a Methodist or a Muslim you go somewhere for the answers to your big questions. Without the collective experience of religion the influence of Jupiter seems more subtle but it is as powerful as any religious practice if and when your beliefs are challenged. Jupiter represents the instinct that gives rise to class action suits, peace marches and NGOs that seek to help where it seems help is not forthcoming from established institutions.

In a study released as a book in 2000 called, *The Cultural Creatives; How 50 Million People Are Changing The World* [5] the authors suggest that there is a kind of non-organized movement of people who do not subscribe to traditional belief systems. These people in their own way, through the books they read, the economic choices they make and the issues and causes they support are culturally creative because they are, in fact, transforming the culture. What motivates their choices is their *belief* that they are choosing the right things, things that they believe in; things like alternative healing, non-traditional ways of educating their children, alternative energy, and a respect for and love of nature. Although many of these people are spiritual and may embrace the practice of spiritual values they often do not feel the need for formal religion. This loosely affiliated, holistic type of thinking is a manifestation of Jupiter's influence in current times—chaotic but nonetheless promising new possibilities to come.

In Western society Jesus Christ is the main symbol for the age of Pisces, the age that is coming to a rather bloody and chaotic end and the ground out of which we are emerging. No matter what our religious background, Christ is an important symbol. Here is an interesting quote for elders at the end of the Age of Pisces.

> *My own idea is that when He comes again it will be to continue His ministry as an old man. I am an old man and my life has been spent as a soldier of Christ, and I tell you that the older I grow the less Christ's teaching says to me. I am sometimes very conscious that I am following the path of a leader who died when he was less than half as old as I am now. I see*

> *and feel things He never saw or felt. I know things He seems never to have known. … am I at fault for wanting a Christ who will show me how to be an old man? All Christ's teaching is put forward with the dogmatism, the certainty, and the strength of youth: I need something that takes account of the accretion of experience, the sense of paradox and ambiguity that comes with years!*—Padre Blazon to Dunstan Ramsey in *Fifth Business* by Robertson Davies [6]

Perhaps we could say that paradox is at the core of duality and duality is at the core of creation. Ambiguity is at the core of how we take action. They are always there in us but even more noticeably as we grow older.

A return of Jupiter asks us to look at what our vision is. The first Jupiter return comes at the age of twelve, at the threshold of adolescence. This first return of Jupiter is significant because every time Jupiter returns after that it will hark back to the first one. At twelve the first collective note of rebellion on the human continuum is heard. This is when we realize that our parents don't know as much as we thought. Of course they know more than we give them credit for but the world has been changing so fast since the mid 18th century that parents don't often know much about the world in which their children will come to adulthood. At twelve the future beckons. "Says who?" becomes something of a mantra. In many faiths this is the age when a person is confirmed as a member of the religion. It is the right age to bring a person into the wider moral construct of the culture. But for those of us for whom this didn't have much meaning or who weren't given the option in the first place we had to go looking for confirmation of our beliefs in the larger world.

Esther remembers at twelve that having a bar mitzvah was the province of boys only. She smiles as she realizes that she didn't question this until she was older and girls began to assume their right to a bat mitzvah as a matter of course. What she does remember is the onset of her menstruation cycle and her mother's anxiety about it. What Esther would have liked was to be welcomed into the secret society of women but what she got was a lot of non-specific anxiety about how she would suffer, bleed and bear children. It was as if her mother wrung her hands in despair as Esther entered womanhood. She definitely was not surprised that her mother called this monthly experience, *the curse.*

Linda, born 11 years later fared differently. She remembers girls around her getting confirmed in their various religious traditions. Her father mocked this and cast suspicion on anyone who believed that such an event had any meaning other than to line the pockets of the priests and ministers. Getting her period was an event Linda was much more informed about than Esther. She and her friends talked about it and her mother was forthcoming with information if not sentiment. Her first rebellion was about shopping. Her parents didn't have money to spare but Linda felt they chose not to share. She found a part-time job so she could buy things her father in particular would disdain and outright disapprove of. Although this was satisfying at twelve by the time she was 24 she traded in shopping for a genuine search for her true values.

Kate experienced her first Jupiter return in the early 70s. What she remembers is her parents conversing about the state of the world. Although she didn't quite understand the larger meaning of things she felt the weight of a world that needed better management and wasn't getting it. She recalls creating a recycling event at her school which seems prophetic of times to come when she looks back on it. Her mother was very encouraging about menstruation. She offered books and real information about the physical and emotional realities of becoming a woman.

The unfortunate thing about not having a community of people who share common beliefs is that at twelve this means you think you can find the truth, the real know-how, in your peers. You find truth in the music and the movies, the popular cultural heroes and the words to songs. Another way in which people meet the needs of Jupiter at the age of twelve and beyond is through sports. People *believe* in their teams and the players. They can have religious types of feelings about winning or losing. It is a short step from the kind of fervor that sports and religion inspire in the human heart to the notion of war. Jupiter, when twisted to its least conscious form is the fanatical belief that only your people are truly human. Nonetheless sports can provide a seemingly moral framework for emerging adolescents but only if the coaches are not predatory or ambitious and the parents don't try to live through their children's abilities.

From these realms a twelve year old learns something other than what their parents have portrayed as *the way we live*. So the challenge begins. Advertising with its driving message of brand loyalty easily becomes something that to the emerging adolescent brain seems to have a deeper message than simply *buy this thing*—even though it doesn't really. True vision in our culture has been slowly and steadily compromised by *spin* especially as it combines with the culture of fear and paranoia that has flourished since 9/11.

As we face the chaos of our times when many communities have no moral center and others are rigidly fundamentalist, it's very difficult to know who is to blame and for what. There are very few filters for the truth. Although this brings up a genuine concern for our children and grandchildren we are also deeply affected by this as elders.

At 60 the landscape is different. The notion that Padre Blazon brings up in the above quote is that as we age we need a belief system that includes a sense of paradox and ambiguity. The younger we are, the easier it is to see things in black and white. Experience is a powerful teacher and combined with the transition of becoming an elder it allows us to see that things are not as clear as we thought. By the time we reach 60 we have had four Jupiter returns and each one has brought us an opportunity to explore the truth as we see it. The first two at twelve and 24 are often about education and/or travel. We need to learn from people who know more than we do even if we suspect they aren't perfect. At 36 and 48 we are in the position to be offering a piece of our mind to those who need guidance. If you are lost there is nothing that will help you find your way more effectively than showing someone else the way. At that stage of our lives we may have offered guidance and moral support to our children, our students or just our friends and peers. The more we are called on to have answers the more we understand that we need to ask the right questions.

We have come a distance since we were twelve and yet we are working out the same core principle. At this stage it isn't our parents who don't know the world in which we live. We may feel that God or the Universe itself is not offering the right kind of guidance. We have serious doubts about the way the system seems to work. Maybe we want to blow the whistle on the moral status quo or maybe we are called to join a religious group in the hope that we will come to understand this world of paradox and ambiguity in which we find ourselves. The sense that someone somewhere has some answers is universal. Maybe we are enthusiastic about what we have learned and feel drawn to inspiring others. Most important at the Jupiter return is the belief that we still have more to learn.

No matter what level of moral development you have achieved at this moment of your life, the Jupiter return suggests that this is a time to reflect upon how much or little distance you have actually traveled from the belief system in which you were raised, and how far you have to go before you feel a personal and authentic connection to truth. The funny thing about truth is that it changes relative to the age and stage of life you are in at any given moment. As Mark Helprin wrote in *A Winter's Tale*: "The beauty of truth is that it need not be proclaimed or believed. It skips from soul to soul, changing form each time it touches, but it is what it is."[7]

Esther looks back at herself at twelve and connects the difficult and confusing messages she received about her body to the wisdom and expertise she has developed on account of her own journey to heal herself of cancer. Not only has she benefited but so have the people around her.

Linda is struck by the fact that her father's rigid, embittered values which poisoned the waters of her childhood also, ironically, gave her a strong sense that her values are a very important starting point for any major choice or contribution she makes to the world. She is pleased by the fact that she seems to have taken her father's fear and mistrust of the world and transformed it into the strength to participate in a painful and difficult world rather than rejection of it.

Kate understands that her awareness of the world at twelve has led her to a sense of taking charge of situations to get the most out of them. She balances a sense of the end justifying the means with a strong belief in the importance of ethical management practices. As she anticipates her Jupiter return at 59 she looks forward to becoming a mentor for people who could benefit from her experience.

As you stand at or reflect upon the significance of the Jupiter return at 60 what is most important is to envision what you believe is possible for you and for the larger world as well. How is it that we can hold a vision of this life that allows for *paradox and ambiguity* which we so instinctively need at this stage of life?

(For an exercise pertaining to Jupiter, see Appendix II: Chapter 4: Jupiter)

Chapter 5

Body and Soul

The full Moon in the night sky is a glorious sight. As children we are fascinated by the way the Moon follows us from a moonlit sky if we catch a glimpse of it through the window as we are driven down a dark road. Humans have been aware of the Moon's light shining in the night since they began to look up at the sky. What we don't always remember is that the Moon shines with reflected light from the Sun. The Moon is always in relationship to the Sun. (Appendix I: Moon phases) When the Moon is new, the Sun and Moon are together in the same place. The Sun's light obscures the Moon and so we cannot see the Moon in the sky at this time. As the Moon moves away from the Sun, the Moon waxes, until, about two weeks after the new Moon, she is directly opposite the Sun and full of light—the full Moon. On the actual day of the full Moon, if the horizon was flat enough you might observe that exactly as the Sun sets in the west, the Moon rises in the east. This remarkable yet commonplace occurrence is an archetypal image of relationship; one person opposite another, shining a light back and forth between them. After the Moon is full, it begins to wane and eventually it finds the Sun again and they begin a new cycle.[1] You can imagine that to the ancients who saw the night sky as a story which reflected life below this cycle of Sun and Moon would have seemed to reflect the archetypal pattern of relationships.

This light that shines between the Sun and Moon is not always a light of love and acceptance. The light of relationship can often be harsh when two people aren't getting along. At these times we have to acknowledge things about ourselves that we'd rather not notice. There is no one like a partner to shine this light on us. The Moon's light can be a challenge to know ourselves more intimately, sometimes through love and other times through strife and challenge.

Every month the Moon and Sun dance across the circle of the sky in an eight phase relationship with one another. When you were born the Moon was in one of these eight phases. The phase under which you were born is a symbolic statement of what stage of relationship the archetypal mother and father were in at the moment of your birth. Symbolically this translates into your perception of your parents' relationship and how you were held within it when you were a child. For better or for worse, our parents' relationship with each other is the first relationship we observe and the one that sets the pattern of our relationships to come. Your Moon phase offers a key to understanding your core relationship style. It suggests how you expect relationship to offer its reflection.

At this point it might be useful to clarify that we are not type-casting the Sun as men and the Moon as women. The phase relationship that the Moon is in with the Sun—new, full or otherwise—is the combined energies of what we might call yin and yang forces within each of us. They are in polarity like day and night or hot and cold. No matter if you are male or female or if your relationships are with the same sex or opposite, the Moon phase reflects where in the dance you are most strongly imprinted.

When a woman comes to an astrologer wanting to know when she might most easily conceive a child, almost every astrologer will look first to the Moon phase the woman was born under. Each month, when the Moon is in that phase, is the best time for her to achieve a pregnancy.[2] We extrapolate from this to say that when the Moon is in the same phase as it was when you were born, it's the best time for creative inspiration in all realms. It is a time when one is most at home and familiar with the balance of yin and yang.

To figure out what phase of the Moon you were born under you need to know the date of your birth. [3] If you have a copy of your astrological chart it would be indicated. As always when working with the material in this book, if you don't have access to your information simply read a description of the eight phases and choose the one that most resonates for you. You will find the keywords for the phases of the Moon in Appendix I.

Once you have figured out your Moon phase and read something about it consider if the Moon was waxing or waning in light when you were born. The waxing Moon (phases one through four) generally indicates a type of person who is discovering and learning how to express and identify herself in this life. Relationships for them are explorations of who they are as well as who the other person might be. The waning Moon (phases five through eight) generally indicates a type of person who has a strong identity and wants to share it with at least one other person. There is less to discover about the 'you' and 'I' of the relationship and more to learn about using the relationship as a container that holds you and your partner together as a unit in the world, perhaps in relationship in the larger community.

Esther was born at the new Moon phase. She is endlessly surprised at how her intensity is not something that other people share. In fact there are times when her intensity is something that other people seem to avoid. She recognizes the pattern of being drawn into relationships by instinct and often wonders, in retrospect, what she could possibly have been thinking. The awareness of having been born at the New Moon helps her to understand why, more than once, she made the choice to be alone rather than to be with someone she perceived as the wrong partner.

Linda was born at the disseminating phase of the Moon. She recognizes a pattern in herself whereby she needs to share her understanding of a situation or experience with her partner. If she can't do this she does not feel connected to the other person. What she has learned as she has matured in relationships is that the intensity of her beliefs can be too much for another person unless it is balanced with their input. Applying this knowledge to her intimate relationships has been as useful personally as it has been professionally. She has learned that although it is important to express her ideas she does not need to compel others to see it her way.

Kate was born at the balsamic phase of the Moon. This is often referred to as the old Moon because it is the last phase before the new cycle. For her a relationship is a place of retreat and renewal. She is not interested in changing her partner but rather she sees the relationship as a place totally unlike the life she lives in the world. She learned early on that bringing her ambitious, efficiency oriented manner to the relationship drove the good feelings away. She is aware of her good fortune in having figured this out for herself as well as in finding a partner who enjoys her style of relationship.

As elders we are not so concerned with our style of relating to others. Husbands, lovers, best friends and children are important to us but the relationship you are most in need of is the one you have with yourself. And just as your parents' relationship set the tone for relationships in your adult life, the relationships of your adult life set the tone for the relationship you will have with yourself as an elder.

This does not mean that if you went through a terrible marriage and a painful divorce that you will somehow have to relive this inside yourself as an elder. At the same time, you are not guaranteed a peaceful old age if you had a long-lasting, loving marriage. When we reflect on the patterns of our past we are engaging in the essential symbolic journey. We are extrapolating from what we know about ourselves and the way we react as well as the things we have experienced to help us consciously orient ourselves to who we might be in the present.

For Esther the idea of using her understanding of the Moon phase to cultivate a relationship with herself inspired her to see that she could champion her intensity and sensitivity to her immediate environment by being aware of how she might best locate herself physically in any given situation. At times this means taking herself to another room, at other times being more fully present to exactly where she is.

As Linda contemplated the challenge of a relationship with herself, knowing how important the notion of sharing her ideas has been, she began to evolve a habit of writing in her journal as if she is writing letters. Sometimes she is writing to herself, sometimes it feels more like letters to the editor of some vast newspaper in the cosmic mind and sometimes she has the distinct feeling that she is speaking to the unborn grandchildren of the world.

When Kate muses on what kind of relationship she might have with herself based on her understanding of her balsamic Moon Phase she is at first frightened that she may have to give up the relationship she has with her partner. Working through this first reaction she realized that in fact all relationships end sooner or later, if not in divorce then in death. Acceptance of this fundamental truth enables her to see that as an elder she would be able to draw on the feeling of unconditional acceptance she feels for and from her husband and allow those feelings to pervade her entire life. She can see that as she must inevitably lay aside her control and ambition in a worldly sense this inner acceptance could become be a great support.

It seems to be a universal truth that the single most important question a person on a spiritual journey asks is, who am I? When we are young this is about our talents and our weaknesses, it is about our self-esteem and how to assert our identity in the world. As we become elders the focus of this question shifts. Now we begin to want to know who is asking the question. If I can ask myself the question, there must be one part of me that asks and another that answers. It's a big question and the door to life's biggest mysteries. One of the greatest spiritual gifts of our elder years is the ever-widening awareness that there can be no answer to the question, even as the need to explore the asking of it becomes more and more important. The phase of the Moon you were born under gives you some indication of how you approach the question, who am I?

A common technique used by astrologers is called *secondary progressions.* Since we are working with symbols, it seems quite plausible for astrologers to say that one day stands for one year. As the Moon cycle takes about twenty-nine days from one new Moon to the next we can say that, by progression, the Moon phase under which you were born returns approximately every twenty-nine years. So whatever phase of the Moon you were born under will return at around the age of twenty-nine at the threshold of your adult life and again around the age of fifty-eight at the threshold of elderhood. This suggests that as we enter our elder years we can know ourselves better through looking at the patterns of our relationships.

What is the nature of this relationship with the self? I believe that the deepest love affair in a person's life is between the body and the soul. They wrap themselves around one another so totally that for a long time we take their relationship for granted. Even if we accept the existence of the soul, we tend to sense this connection more than we know it. Unless we are of a mystical bent we generally take the relationship between the body and the soul for granted.

In times of personal or collective difficulty, when we are frightened and in pain, we reach for this connection. We long and yearn to feel "at one" with our self. In that longing we know instinctively that the relationship with our inner beloved is the door in, the way we will come to know our soul. In these times of global chaos that surround our lives and sometimes touch us directly, the search for the soul has become much more common than it once was.

Many of us have spent a great deal of time and energy searching for our one true soul mate in another, only to come to the realization that, no matter how deep the love we might share, we must address the body/soul relationship within each of us. I think this is one of the most crucial awakenings that can occur as we enter the elder realm. There is very little of authentic value in our dominant materialistic culture that encourages us to seek the inner relationship.

I am always amused by the beautiful and often wordy ads featured in spirituality magazines. The irony is that to actually have this relationship with the self one must put down the book, the magazine, one must unplug, so to speak, and find a place within which is deeper than the mind; a place that lives outside the need for one more sacred object or meaningful experience. There is a profound need to let go, which, much to the dismay of a consumer society, implies that nothing need be added.

The body/soul love affair is constantly interrupted by the mind. The threshold of elderhood distresses the mind as does all profound change in a person's life. At twenty-eight you needed to orient yourself to your position in the world. At fifty-nine you need to "dis-orient," because true North can only be found within. There is no way to orient outside the self. As we journey inevitably deeper into our aging, worldly things begin very gradually to hold us less and less.

We seem to have an instinctive longing to develop this quality of inner relationship as we get older. Instinctively we know that awareness of and possible fulfillment of this relationship is within reach as we age. This doesn't mean we don't need and appreciate our mate if we have one, our hobbies, families or gardens. It suggests that our experience of these things is tempered by an inner awareness. In astrology things often come in threes. The first great connection we have is with our mother, for security and comfort; the second is with a mate, for intimacy and the children that may come from that; the third great connection is with the soul, for inner security, comfort and knowledge.

In no way am I attempting to define the meaning of the word *soul* here. Let us just say for the sake of this journey that it is the part of us that lives on after we die. It is the part of us that comes from the other world and is apparently invisible, although we do sense it when we look into the eyes of another. You know what the word *soul* means to you and that is the best definition.

I would like to make a distinction between spirit and soul, however. In spirit we are all one. We are all the same. The soul is actually a personal aspect of the identity, a reflection of our body/mind that lives both in the manifest as well as the unmanifest realm of our being. Perhaps the soul is akin to the image of a traditionally devoted wife. She stays home and waits for the body/mind to return from a day's work or perhaps a lifetime's work and share what it has learned because she can only learn through the experiences of the body/mind. She is shaped and molded by the experiences of the body/mind. At night when we lie down, she is the voice that helps us sort through the experiences of the day. She, in a way, makes it all worthwhile. If we don't bring our experience to this aspect of ourselves it's a kind of betrayal of the soul.

Whether you like it or not, this relationship of the body/mind and the soul cannot end in divorce—only in death. As we become elders one thing that becomes clear is that we have less time. Quite literally our sense of time is different than it used to be. Time seems to go by faster. When you were born a day was 100 percent of your life. When you were two days old it was 50 percent. By now one day is quite a small percentage of your life. The mind perceives time based on this. So here we are, life is speeding by and we still have not done totally right by the soul. There is still something more that this relationship needs.

Life is generous. As the body/mind goes through time it changes, which means the quality of experience changes and therefore there are *always* new and different things to learn. As the saying goes, you can never step into the same river twice. There is a strong possibility that in this life, no matter what age you are, there is always something new coming along. The love affair between the body and the soul is always evolving.

The relationship our culture has to the body is a difficult one. One of the most basic mandates of traditional Western society is that nature must be subdued. Our relationship to our physical body reflects the larger relationship of society to the planet. The funny thing about the body or perhaps nature in general, both of which can be known by the senses, is that it has a very strong connection to the unconscious, which lies buried deep below the realm of our senses. When difficult things happen to us, the conscious mind may forget, but the body will store the memory deep in our unconscious. The opposite is also true. An experience of great joy may not be in your mind but if you catch the scent of something that was present at the same time as you experienced that joy, memories will come flooding back. People generally are willing to remember their joy without blocking it but often we would rather not be reminded of our pain and so the body becomes a storehouse of suffering which, as we age, manifests in "dis-ease." As Alice Miller, the Swiss expert on childhood trauma wrote in *The Drama of the Gifted Child*:

> The truth about our childhood is stored up in our body and although we can repress it, we can never alter it. Our intellect can be deceived, our feelings manipulated, our conceptions confused, and our body tricked with medication. But someday the body will present its bill, for it is as incorruptible as a child who, still whole in spirit, will accept no compromises or excuses, and it will not stop tormenting us until we stop evading the truth. [4]

It is important when handling such a concept that you don't think of yourself as guilty of some misdeed should you have an illness. If, for example a person is unfortunate enough to have a disease it does not mean that she caused it by her thoughts and feelings in any direct way. More useful is to understand that if the stomach is sick our soul is speaking through the body and telling us that we have trouble feeling cared for and nourished. If our heart has problems the soul eloquently suggests we have issues about love. Despite the fact that we may not always enjoy it, it is a conversation with one's most intimate partner. It is not a judgment, blaming the victim for having a problem. We can also converse in less difficult ways with our soul through meditation or writing in a journal or creating art of any kind. In fact, all that we manifest in material reality is, in one way or another, an expression of our soul. You don't exist apart from the larger world in which you live and there is only so much a person can do to become awakened to these truths. The more we are aware of the connections between our unconscious and the expression of our bodies, the more we learn and the freer we can become.

We have a sense of this in Esther's story of how developing cancer in her forties led to an amazing amount of self-discovery, which she benefited from for the rest of her life. For Linda these body/soul issues manifest most clearly in her intimate relationships with men. Her sexual history tells the story of what her body remembers. Kate's awareness of this grew considerably when in her 40s her career direction shifted from high up on the corporate ladder to self-employed. In the period of transition she understood how working for the bosses had burned her out physically, emotionally and mentally. She realized that in working for herself she would be able to include essential times of self-care. Simple as this may appear it meant that she began to understand herself as the one great resource of her life.

The more we listen to, accept and love our body, the simpler our needs get. In a consumer culture, however, the message is that if you love your body you will buy this thing and that thing because you *deserve* it. And if your body frightens or disgusts you, you will keep throwing things at it so you don't have to hear what it says. By the time we become elders we need to know when we have had enough. There most likely isn't one more *thing* that is going to make us happy. We need to look deeper within ourselves.

This is when the love between the body and the soul is really put to the test. This is when that love can really mature.

People often ask me if they are a young soul or an old soul. The assumption is somehow that old souls are smarter and more spiritually developed than younger ones. That makes sense in a rational way, but I'm not sure the soul really conforms to rational thinking. For our purposes on this journey, we might think of the soul as ageless. The soul changes through time based on experiences and learning, but it is the body that shows the signs of age—not the soul. I don't know if it ever was young, and I don't know how to evaluate if it is old. Maybe what we mean by an old soul is really a wise soul, one that has actually learned from its time here on earth. In *The Portrait of Dorian Gray,* the body stays young and the soul grows evil, and only the portrait tells the tale. Perhaps Oscar Wilde was onto something in that if the body doesn't grow old, the soul can't grow wise.

Derek Walcott, the Nobel Prize-winning West Indies poet and playwright, wrote this poem in his late forties:

"LOVE AFTER LOVE"
BY DEREK WALCOTT

The time will come when,
with elation,
you will greet yourself arriving
at your own door, in your own mirror,
and each will smile at the other's welcome,

and say, sit here. Eat.
You will love again the stranger who was your self.
Give wine. Give bread. Give back your heart
to itself, to the stranger who has loved you

all your life, whom you ignored
for another, who knows you by heart.
Take down the love letters from the bookshelf,

the photographs, the desperate notes,
peel your own image from the mirror.
Sit. Feast on your life. [5]

Most of us have an image of how we look, based on how others have seen us through our lives. It is the rare woman who doesn't feel that her hair is too curly or too straight, her breasts or butt are too big or too small, ad infinitum. Even a woman who is considered a beauty in this culture may be reduced to a commodity and not view her own beauty as an expression of something inner.

The most touching irony lives in the fact that when we look back to how we appeared at twenty-nine, at the threshold of our adult lives, we are almost all struck by how beautiful we were just because we were young (although we may not have felt beautiful back then). Perhaps the same is true for this stage of our lives. If we get to look back at ourselves at sixty from the vantage point of ninety, chances are that we would think we looked pretty good back then.

(For an exercise pertaining to your Moon phase, go to Appendix II: Chapter 5: Moon Phase.)

PSYCHE, EROS AND VENUS

For the purpose of our journey into elderhood let us say there are two aspects to the soul. The Moon and her phases represent the repository of our memories and describe our relationship patterns, as discussed above. The Moon is about mother. Then there is Venus: Beauty Herself. Venus tells us of our connection to beauty, love and what we cherish or value in this life. The symbol for Venus is the circle of spirit balanced or attached to the cross of matter: ♀ Perhaps the symbol of Venus represents matter seducing spirit or perhaps it is about the intense longing that spirit has to be embodied.

As the representation of values Venus is often misinterpreted. In a consumer society our values are cultivated and created outside the self. We are led to believe that one thing has value for everyone and something else has none. Actual authentic perception of value is about pleasure, not ethics. Our values as well as our understanding of value itself are learned very young, through our senses. If we are thwarted from exploring the world in this manner as young children we are forever confused about what our values are and so we try to make sense of them from outside. We come to believe what we are told about what has true value. We gradually lose the ability to know from within ourselves and without doubt what it is we value. When we buy something expensive such as a car or a piece of furniture or even a work of art simply because others are buying the same thing it can be a great disappointment to discover that it has lost its value. Of course if we buy any one of these things because we genuinely love it, then it hardly matters if it goes out of fashion or gets devalued in the marketplace. [6]

A person whose values are grounded in their senses would not likely have any inclination to destroy the environment in which they live. Beauty in all its manifestations would be as important as function. Venus has everything to do with the five senses, the gateways of perception. My guess is that if we were culturally more inclined to perceiving the world from within the subjective realm of our senses, if we were allowed as children to distinguish our preferences and dislikes without the manipulative overlay of advertising we would be less likely to do harm to one another as well as to the planet. We might be a much gentler species if we paid attention to what smells good, what tastes good, what feels good, what looks good and what sounds good. Out of these very senses, common to all undoubtedly arise the true notion of common sense which is the domain of Venus.

Generally speaking things are more beautiful and smell better when they are young, fresh, full. So what about Venus for the elders? As we grow into being elders the need for beauty becomes more important. We often grow into a deeper appreciation for the arts whether we are experiencing the works of others or expressing ourselves in some way. It's as if the soul cries out for a reflection of itself. In *Beauty: The Invisible Embrace,* John O'Donohue says:

> In a sense, all the contemporary crises can be reduced to a crisis about the nature of beauty. This perspective offers us new possibilities. . . . When we address difficulty in terms of the call to beauty, new invitations come alive. Perhaps, for the first time, we gain a clear view of how much ugliness we endure and allow. The media generate relentless images of mediocrity and ugliness . . . The media are becoming the global mirror and . . . enshrine the ugly as the normal standard.
>
> There is an unseemly coarseness to our times, which robs the grace from our textures of language, feeling and presence. Such coarseness falsifies and anaesthetizes our desire. . . . Greed is unable to envisage any form of relationship other than absorption or possession. However, when we awaken to beauty, we keep desire alive in its freshness, passion and creativity.
>
> It has become the habit of our times to mistake glamour for beauty . . . No one ever catches up to glamour. . . . Glamour has but a single flicker. In contrast, the Beautiful offers us an invitation to order, coherence and unity. When these needs are met, the soul feels at home in the world." [7]

As elders our soul has the option to discover that time's greatest gift comes when we are aware of ourselves in the present. Although we are conditioned by the past and anticipating the future we always have the option to be fully alive in the moment. Our bodies inevitably slow down. Beauty is more readily appreciated when we have greater peace and stillness within. Feeling beautiful ourselves becomes less important than our ability to perceive beauty in the world around us with our senses.

Here is a myth about Venus and beauty. In myth we are often able to apprehend the essential archetypal qualities of the human condition. Astrology uses the myths of the ancients to find clues as to the meanings of the planets. Any myth about Venus the Goddess is relevant to our understanding of the symbolic meaning which Venus may offer astrologically.

Generally this story is told as the story of Psyche (which means "Soul") and Eros (which means a particular kind of love—erotic love). As you read the story consider the perspective of Venus. The inspiration for this comes from a morning just before my sixtieth birthday when I was meditating on nothing particular and the question arose in my mind, *What good is Venus to an old lady?*

This story speaks of the deep need that the Soul has for Love itself. It has had an enormous impact on fairy tales for a couple of thousand years. You will see traces of Beauty and the Beast, as well as many others. [8]

Once upon a time, Venus was the undisputed beauty of heaven and earth. For about nine months at a time she could be seen in the evening sky and recognized as the most beautiful heavenly orb. If she touched a man his heart would burst open with love for the next woman he saw. If she graced a woman with her aura there would be hell to pay because heavenly beauty in a woman is something that men and women long to possess and keep forever. We all know the story of Helen of Troy. On her seashell throne this makes Venus laugh. She knows that there is absolutely nothing that humans can possess forever. And she enjoys her place as the most beautiful goddess in the universe.

One terrible day, Venus becomes aware that many people have stopped coming to worship in her temples. There is a young woman—the daughter of a king and queen, the youngest of three sisters and the most beautiful mortal woman ever to be born. Her name is Psyche. Her beauty is so great that people actually stop praying to Venus, taking Psyche for the Goddess of Beauty incarnate. This enrages Venus. She is filled with the heavenly urge to get revenge on someone who so blatantly challenges her place.

"So much for me, the ancient mother of nature, primeval origin of the elements, Venus, nurturer of the whole world: I must go halves with a mortal girl in the honor due to my godhead, and my name, established in heaven, is profaned by earthly dirt! It seems that I am to be worshipped in common and that I must put up with the obscurity of being adored by deputy, publicly represented by a girl—a being who is doomed to die! . . . But she will rue the day, whoever she is, when she usurped my honors. I'll see to it that she regrets this beauty of hers, to which she has no right." [9]

In the typical manner of jealousy, Venus goes after innocent Psyche who cannot really be blamed for her beauty. She commands her son Eros to make Psyche fall in love with the ugliest, nastiest man on Earth. Eros, who has done jobs like this on his mother's behalf before, goes down to Earth with his magic arrows to find Psyche.

Eventually Eros finds her, asleep in a meadow. As he stands over her sleeping form he is struck not only by her beauty but by the purity of her inner being. Eros bends down toward Psyche and accidentally pierces himself with his own arrow and so his love for her blossoms. At once he flies away because, as we all know, mortals cannot mate with immortals. But he cannot control his feelings of love for her.

After a while Venus realizes that Eros's magic is not working as she can see that Psyche is not falling in love with anyone, let alone someone hideous. Psyche figures out that she is somehow cursed by her beauty. Through no intention or action of her own, she has drawn the animosity of a goddess in a very personal way. As Psyche's sorrow grows it becomes clear that she will marry no one. Oracles are consulted and she is brought to a high mountaintop and abandoned to her fate.

From the mountaintop she is carried off in her sleep by the gentle west wind and delivered to a beautiful grassy knoll. When she awakes, she does not see a horrible monster but rather a beautiful fountain in front of what could only be a magical castle. Then she hears a voice, telling her that the castle is hers, and the invisible servants around her are there to do her bidding. Delighted and relieved she walks through the castle and finds many wonderful things. At last she is tired and hungry and before she can even ask a beautiful breakfast is laid out before her. That evening the castle grows dark and a new voice speaks to her. This voice is kind and loving, and she can't imagine that it is that of a monster. The voice says he is her husband. Although she begs him to let her see him he sadly refuses, telling her that the day she sees him is the day their happiness comes to an end. So they live their strange marriage in this way: she is alone all day and at night, in a dark room, they share their love.

Although Eros is very kind and loving, Psyche is not happy because her days are spent so alone. One day her sisters come to visit. They are jealous of the incredible riches and beauty that surrounds Psyche. They convince her that her husband must be a monster, waiting only to kill her one evening when she least suspects it. She must take a lamp and a knife into the bedroom and if in the lamplight she sees a terrible monster she must kill him. What she sees of course is beautiful Eros with his mighty wings. Their eyes meet. Their love bursts into a more intense passion and he vanishes and with him the castle and the life they shared.

Venus is pleased with this turn of events, but one day the most wretched Psyche comes to her temple, longing to find her husband. She will not give up her love, but now she must face a terrible adversary who only wishes her dead and gone. Psyche implores Venus to restore her marriage. Venus offers tasks assuming each time that the task at hand will finish Psyche off. Each time Psyche returns ready to do whatever she must to win her Eros back.

The first task is the sorting of a mountain of different seeds. Psyche cannot do this on her own. She falls asleep and the ants come and do it for her.

The second task is to steal a strand of Golden Fleece from the fierce rams on the other side of the river. Desperate and ignorant of the dangers of the task Psyche steps into the river. Suddenly she hears the voices of the river spirits who tell her how dangerous the rams are and that they will tear her apart. She must wait until night falls and looks for the golden threads while they are asleep. Once again she is successful.

For the third task Venus gives Psyche a crystal jar and demands she fill it from the mountain peak where the river Styx, guarded by dragons, emerges from Hades, the land of death. Although Psyche makes the climb up to the entrance of the cave the dragons are much to be feared. To her relief Zeus sends an eagle that completes this task for her

The last and most difficult task is one that Venus is certain will vanquish Psyche because no human can return from the land of the dead. She orders Psyche to go to Queen Persephone of the Underworld and request a pot of magical beauty cream. At this point Psyche is ready to admit defeat but she is strangely willing throughout the story to die if she must. So she sets off for the underworld. True to the wonders of love down through the ages she is prompted by a voice—the voice of her true love and husband, Eros, but she doesn't know that—who tells her she must bring coins for the ferryman and barley cakes for the three-headed dog. She must use one coin and three cakes going in and coming out.

Venus is certain that this task will kill Psyche in the end. And then she will finally be free of the insult that the beauty of this mere mortal causes her. Psyche descends with great trepidation into the underworld. It is dark and dank. She is filled with equal parts despair and longing. She doubts everything about this quest she is on—especially herself. At last she comes to the encounter with the Queen of the Dead. She is surprised by the kindness and mercy that flow from Persephone toward her and the willingness with which she provides the pot of magical beauty cream.

Calmed and restored Psyche makes her way back to the upper world. As she trudges across the terrain toward Venus's temple she is overcome by the idea that she should take a dab of beauty cream for herself. Who would know after all? Quite likely she isn't looking as good as she once did, due to all the stress and strain of questing in difficult circumstances.

As she touches the cream to her face, she instantly falls down dead. At this point the gods take pity on her. She is rescued, brought up to Mt. Olympus, made into an immortal and reunited with Eros. Venus will just have to work it out and so she does. [10]

Unfortunately that is not how the story goes for many of us. I think we might learn something as elders if we look not so much at the love of Psyche and Eros but rather at the difficulty between Venus and Psyche. The mother (in-law) / daughter relationship is core to understanding many things. Although we don't all have daughters, we are all daughters. And each of us, as we approach our elder years is aware of the terrible truth that beauty is wasted on the young! It is likely that, just as Parzival was not able to liberate the grail castle until he was a grown man, with many years of experience, that by the time Psyche finished these tasks she too was much older and somewhat, if not completely, wiser than she was at the beginning.

Now let us take myth and mix it with some astronomical information. Venus spends about nine months in an 18 month period being either the morning or evening star. There are times when she disappears from the sky all together. Various myths deal with the issue of Venus not being visible in the sky. The myths and stories that have grown up around this astronomical event are about the goddess descending into the underworld. Generally it is considered that these are not good times for love.

One of the most fascinating things about the cycles of Venus is that if you plot the positions of Venus vanishing from the night sky over an eight-year period and then connect the dots on a circle you get a perfect pentacle. This kind of geometric symmetry is the very stuff of beauty.

In the chart of an individual, Venus will return to the exact place she was in when you were born every year; much less frequently, she will also return at the same time as the Sun returns to a place close to where it was when you were born. Generally this occurs in eight-year intervals but this can vary somewhat. In your fifties you will experience one or two of these Venus/Sun returns.

If we want to figure out what good Venus might be to an old lady, we might consider how and if we have fulfilled the four tasks that Psyche was given when she was young and beautiful. Thinking symbolically we know that four is the number of orientation. It grounds us as in the four directions. Contemplating these four tasks may help to orient our awareness of how the soul is anchored to the body/mind. (Appendix II: Chapter 5 exercises: Venus.)

The first task is about discrimination. Psyche must sort but she cannot do it without the help of the most industrious and organized of insects, the ant. This suggests to me that she must give up relying upon her judgment to figure out the whys of her predicament. It is too great a task to figure out the right and wrong of her situation. She must reach into a more basic sense—perhaps her common sense—and just put the seeds where they belong, not where she thinks they *should* belong. The ants represent a basic physical aspect of her that knows how to do this.

The second task requires that she wait till nightfall when the rams are asleep but that she needs to be awake in the night. Since the ram is a symbol of Aries and Aries is associated with the fierce passion of individuality we might conjecture that Psyche must wait until her passionate identification with her plight is asleep and then look for the gold. Passion flourishes where reason is absent. If Psyche would be reunited with Love, her passion must sleep, but there is gold to be had if she can stay awake and aware.

The third task requires more courage than the first two. There is nothing scary about seeds and Psyche was ignorant of the danger of the rams. Planning to climb a mountain and face dragons takes a certain amount of fortitude. Psyche is rewarded for her bravery by the visitation of an eagle from Zeus himself. The eagle is a strong and majestic animal that can see from a far distance. As a messenger from Zeus it represents vision itself. Crystal is also a symbol of clarity, and water from the underworld might represent the deep and powerful feelings that arise when we experience loss such as Psyche feels at the loss of Eros.

The last task is truly the most supernatural one because it is impossible to return from the land of the dead if you are mortal. By accomplishing this successfully, Psyche proves that she is more than mortal. She is guided by Eros to find the wisdom which will enable her return, not to mention that she has the blessing of the Queen of Death as she willingly parts with a little pot of beauty. Psyche does not have to use manipulation or tricks to secure this treasure. By the time our heroine gets to this task she has learned how to discriminate without blame, she has faced down the passion of her identity, she has learned about loss and therefore compassion. Clearly she is ready to look upon the face of her own death and live. As we become elders we are asked to do something similar. And the reward is the same. We can possibly appease the Queen of Heaven, Beauty Herself, and be united in soul and body if we can accept that all things mortal end and that there is a part of us that is not mortal even if we aren't sure what that part is.

Such is the wisdom of myth that at the very last, when Psyche has almost achieved her ultimate goal, she is overcome by a desire to have a little beauty cream for herself. It is vanity that propels her. She is concerned that all her travails have made her look less beautiful, that Eros will not still love her. She doubts herself. She convinces herself that Venus will not know if she takes a dab for herself. Such is the way of humans. We achieve cosmic things only to be undone by our simple human appetites and foibles. But nonetheless she is loved, saved, exalted and redeemed.

It's almost impossible to connect body and soul without poetry. Poetry seems to speak to the body as well as the soul at the same time. This poem which suggests to me the love of soul and body/mind is from a collection called *Wild Dogs* by Helen Humphreys: [11]

I lay down in the tall meadow grasses.
I lay down in the fragrant song of earth.
I lay down in the polish of the morning and the tarnish of the evening.
I lay down in rain.
I lay down under the word as promise and the word as deed.
I lay down alone.
I lay down in the hollows made by ice and rock and filled each year with winter.
I lay down on the hard stone bed of grief.
I lay down with the taste of Sunlight on my skin, with summer in my mouth, with a veil of bees around my hair.
I lay down with dying in my bones.
I lay down under the sweet, anxious sorrow of you.

I rise up from water, from air, from the hard body of earth.
I rise up into memory, into springtime, into all I once held by name.
I rise up with hope for the new day.
I rise up in mourning.
I rise up with the taste of loss bitter on my tongue and your name still warm on my skin.
I rise up from the soft, dark room of sleep, blank as water.
I rise up with the whispered secrets of the insects a woven lace above my eyes.
I rise up.
(Say it.)
I rise up from your body for the last time.

Esther tells of how she experienced the changes in her body in her sixties. She grew up believing that she was beautiful even if this was not worth much to her as far as bringing love into her life. Her mother would tell stories about how perfect strangers would stop them on the street when Esther was a baby just to look upon her beautiful daughter. Esther grew up proud of her looks at a time when the greatest asset a woman could have was beauty. This may be a perennial truth but from Esther's perspective the wave of feminism that washed over the world of women in the seventies brought a sea change in the way women viewed their physical bodies. She took great advantage of this by embracing the value of yoga and health. She began to feel her beauty in quite a different way than she had before. Nonetheless at around the age of sixty a terrible sadness came over her. Even having discovered the women's movement and the exhilaration of freedom from many of the things that distort the natural image of women, as an elder she looked in the mirror, she looked down at her body and she felt betrayed by what she saw as her ruined beauty. The body seemed to have betrayed her and her soul couldn't find a comfortable place. For a time it was as if the values of her early days rose up and engulfed her, washing away all the triumph and power of womanhood that she had experienced in between.

For Linda who is at this writing only on the verge of her elder years the sense of herself as losing her beauty is different. She was shocked one day when she compared herself in a photo at 50 to a similar one at 60. The difference was astounding and one she hadn't realized. Up until that moment she had thought she looked basically the same as she had at 50. Not so! At 50 she looked like a slightly older version of herself at 30 by 60 she looked quite different all together. In a way she likes the sense that as she gets older and less beautiful in an outward way her relationships with men may come to be based on who she really is inside rather than how she looks. This could be something to look forward to.

There are many who feel betrayed by the changes that age brings to the body even as they suspect the possibility of a different kind of beauty that lifts them up—grace. Gravity and grace are another loving couple that we contend with all our lives on planet Earth. Gravity holds us to Earth even as it pulls us down and eventually helps our skin to sag. Grace gives us wings. Is this true love then if they are such polar opposites? And is love always connected to beauty so that when love dies we feel ugly or when beauty leaves we cannot love ourselves anymore? Maybe it was easier back in the day when there were no mirrors. Then you could only see yourself or approximate what you might look like by looking at someone else. It's easy to see beauty in the ones we love no matter how age has marked them. Love is the key that lets beauty shine through. Therefore it is clear what we must do to preserve our beauty till the end. We must love. If we were magicians we could put love in little pots of cream and dab it on our skin but it would work better if we dabbed it on each other. "There is no private salvation; exchange with the other is the door to the final awareness of the unity of all in the love which is the dance of creation." [12]

My mother loved Dorothy Parker. She loved to tell me the story about a younger more beautiful woman holding the door for Ms. Parker who said, "Age before beauty" as she opened the door. "Pearls before swine" was Dorothy's reply. It is quite possible that this incident never actually happened. But I know that as unattractive as my mother always thought she was, the worst thing for her was aging. It ruined the beauty she never believed she had in the first place. And she was ashamed. So she had a facelift. And they botched it. This was ruined beauty. I wanted my mother's face to age simply because I loved her. I felt very upset that I didn't get to see her real face change as she got older.

As a young and unwrinkled woman I felt she had ruined her beauty. She defiled the face of the Mother—my mother. From the perspective of an older, weathered woman I understand on many levels why she did what she did. She couldn't see love in her face as she aged because when she looked in the mirror she saw her mother. Better for her to disfigure that face than to become her mother!

One of the strangest things for me personally about growing older is how much I see my parents in my face when I look in the mirror. No one else sees them but me. I am fortunate in that I feel no impulse to ruin what I see. This must be progress. And you, when you study the lines on your face in the mirror, do you see the face of a beloved or difficult parent? Can you tolerate the notion that this may possibly be a message from your soul?

(For exercises pertaining to Venus, see Appendix II: Chapter 5: Venus. To deepen the connection between the Moon Phase and Venus see The Love Affair exercise directly following.)

KARMIC PATHS: HABITS VS. FREEDOM

To the symbolic eye of human beings down through the ages the Sun and Moon have come to represent the archetypal powers and rhythms of god and goddess, mother and father, king and queen. These are primary constructs in the psyche. Any information we can find about the way the Sun and Moon connect to one another is significant. So far we have explored the phase relationship between the Sun and the Moon but there is yet another way we can see the dance of these great luminaries through what we call the Nodes of the Moon. The North and South Nodes of the Moon are quite different than the eight phases of the Moon (which we have worked with above) in that they are not visible to the naked eye. Perhaps this is why astrologers have ascribed to them a more subtle and occult meaning. For our purposes in this exploration we can say that the Nodes are the way the Sun and Moon connect out in more distant space. (For a more detailed explanation, see Appendix I: Nodes) The eight phases of the Moon tell us about our style of relationship which is something we can observe in our day to day life. The Nodes tell us about our unconscious habits and the lessons we need to learn to become more awake and aware to our overall behavior.

Even though Nodes are not planets they do have a return cycle that takes about nineteen years. These returns occur at around age nineteen, thirty-eight and fifty-seven. (Appendix I: Nodes)

The Nodes are not planets, they are points in space. Symbolically this means they do not symbolize relationships with people in your life so much as to patterns within you. As we learned above, the Moon represents your mother. If we want to know about your relationship to your mother, we can look at the placement of the Moon in your chart. If we want to know more about your Moon, we can ask you about your relationship to your mother. Think of the nodes more as portals or points in the psyche rather than people.

In Vedic astrology they tell a story about the Nodes.[13] One day the Lord of all the gods gathered them together so that they might drink the nectar of immortality. A demon who had disguised himself as a god snuck into this meeting and managed to drink some of the nectar. As he did so, the Sun and the Moon recognized him and the great Lord of the gods cut the demon in half with his golden disc. Alas it was too late to prevent the demon from becoming immortal. From that moment forward the two halves of the demon became the arch enemies of the Sun and the Moon. We know this because whenever there is an eclipse of the Sun or Moon they are near the Nodes. An eclipse was thought to be a great dragon devouring the heavenly lights. The North Node is often referred to as the dragon's head and the South Node as the dragon's tail.

The core concept of the Nodes is that the South Node tells of our unconscious patterns or karma and the North Node tells us where we must reach to grow in awareness of these patterns. When we hear the word karma, most of us immediately think of past lives and bad deeds. Karma in the sense we will use here isn't simply about all the bad things you have done. Karma is actually more pervasive than that. It's everything you've ever done—good or bad—that you are still attached to. It's unfinished business, both joyful and miserable. It sticks to you in the way of memory and habit. You do not have to *believe* in past lives to look at the Nodes. You simply have to believe that you have a past that affects your present. Because astrology is the study of cycles, the notion that we are continuous beings is an easy metaphor to use to explain things. When I refer to past lives, I am using the concept metaphorically, not religiously.

Imagine that in a past life you abandoned your children. You knew it was wrong, you felt terrible about it but circumstances gave you no choice. In this life you might still have a sense of guilt or fear that you will abandon the ones you love because you have not come to a place of forgiveness in yourself, which would have allowed you to let go of the guilt. If you had made amends and experienced forgiveness at a level that allows you to let go, you would not need to deal with those feelings again in this life. Karma might be the love you had for a friend who died young that you never stopped missing. If, however, you finally found enough peace to let your friend go and no longer felt attached to the sadness or the loss, you would then no longer have that karma or the habit of feeling that you endlessly miss someone.

As the South Node tells us of our habits or karma, the North Node suggests a way to help break with habit and become aware of our actions. There is usually a level of discomfort with the North Node and a sense of familiarity with the South Node.

The first time your Nodes return at around eighteen or nineteen the message is that this is *your* life. No matter who did what to you, this is going to be *your* experience. People can offer suggestions but no one can actually live your life for you. It's a major step toward ultimately becoming fully adult. In Western culture it might be about leaving high school (mandatory education) and striking off on the path of higher education (formal or not) on your own. The idea here isn't about education it's about the fact that the path is not ordained unless you ordain it. Obviously people have more or less awareness of this. When I do charts for new parents I tell them that there is nothing they need to do to make the North Node easier for their child. The very essence of it is that you must find it on your own. It will be up to the child to figure this one out when they are older. Of course what a parent can do is to help a child with the South Node by fostering habits that are healthy and not compulsive.

At thirty-eight the Nodes return again and the message is slightly different. Now you have been an adult for a while. You have, or have not, achieved the material direction you want. This ushers in mid-life crises and it's a time to adjust your path. It is a kind of karmic wake-up call.

In your fifties you get another chance for some deep reflection about how the past holds you and where the comfort zone ends. Once again you must lean into the place of possible discomfort that leads toward growth. Now you are more aware than ever of how the conditioning of your early life has helped create your reality. With hindsight it is easy to see how one makes choices based, not on what lies ahead but rather on what you learned from the past. Although you can't slip off your habits like an old coat you might be tired of repeating old patterns. What is offered to us when the Nodes return in our 50s is the possibility of recognizing that habits and the things we do automatically are clearly just that—automatic responses. We are not striving to have no habits. We are attempting to recognize them for what they are and become more accepting of the growing edge. The North Node is your growing edge. (Appendix II: exercises for the Nodes)

For Esther the return of her Nodes brought a difficult and significant situation. She was in the habit of caring and sacrificing for those around her in greater need than herself. At around that time a good friend began to lean heavily on Esther to help her fight a terrible battle with breast cancer. Given the work she had done as well as the knowledge she had accumulated on the journey of healing her own cancer, Esther felt compelled to offer everything she had to her friend. After a few months of this Esther began to get ill. She developed symptoms that would simply not leave. Understanding that her karmic habit from the past was to sacrifice herself without boundaries to the needs of others Esther began to make clear, strong and serious boundaries for herself. Although this meant being less available to her friend it meant being stronger and more able to be fully present when they were together.

When Linda's Nodes returned she was caught in a gossip triangle with her financial planner. If it hadn't been so embarrassing it would have been funny. Catty comments, lost checks, misunderstandings and most of all rampant judgments and assumptions blew up in her face, almost destroying her relationships with a good friend as well as her financial advisor. Once things got straightened out Linda realized in that profound way that life offers for our most significant lessons that had she simply listened and refrained to comment everyone would have worked out their issues minus the entanglement.

Kate looks back to her node return in her late 30s. This was around the time when her office was downsizing. When she was let go she felt like a sacrificial lamb. This did not happen because of her level of performance, in fact she was a high performer, but more on account of the fact that she was younger than many of those at the same level and a woman who might, in their eyes, at any moment decide to take care of her mother or move to a foreign country with her husband. Given that none of these things was actually happening Kate was furious and then deeply hurt. Eventually she emerged from the ashes of this wounding experience. She found herself with time to care for herself, some interesting ideas about how to move forward and a sizable package. Finally she realized that although she had been let go for all the wrong reasons in the end it was a small miracle to be offered the option to start again in a better way. She hopes if something akin to this happens in her 50s she will look for the blessing in the transformation right at the beginning.

The Nodes present us with a life-long challenge to catch ourselves in the act of being unconscious, but they also suggest a way to channel that energy and thereby to evolve spiritually. If liberation is the goal—always strived for, not necessarily achieved—then anything that helps us let go of unconscious attachment moves us toward awareness. The subtle piece at work when dealing with the Nodes is that there is a huge difference between non-attachment and disconnection. Non-attachment is laced with compassion and a willingness to experience whatever life has to offer without holding on to it. Disconnection is denial. The former embraces life, the latter negates it.

If you despise your unconscious habits—your excessive love of chocolate or shopping—you will want to exorcize them from your life as if they aren't yours. If you cultivate an awareness of your habits as you are doing them, you have a much greater chance of integrating that awareness into a greater comfort level with the suggestions presented by North Node or in simply finding a natural balance.

At 19 the Node return asks us to adjust the material or circumstantial path we are on. At 38 the return suggests an emotional adjustment is necessary. In our 50s the Nodes require a mental adjustment which allows us to accept that there actually is a next stage of development—our elder years. We come to the understanding that there is a difference between our adult and elder years. In our mid-70s the Nodes offer a spiritual understanding of our karmic patterns. No matter what sign or house they are in the challenge here is to understand at a deep level that the story of our lives is a metaphor for all life. The South Node is the portal through which we entered this life. The North Node is the one through which we will ultimately leave. Every 19 years we have the opportunity to practice.

The Nodes are not so much about the ongoing love affair between the body and the soul. They don't tell us about our parents. They are more about the initial attraction that calls the soul to be born into a body in the first place. They speak of our descent into matter; the taking on of a body because we still have so much to learn from the unfinished business of the past. The Nodes represent the lessons we must still learn and possible ways to learn them. They seem to call out a feeling akin to falling in love rather than the process of working something out. As anyone who has ever been in a relationship knows, love tends to bring up the things that need healing. The Nodes show us what those things might be. The Moon phase is the ongoing process by which we do it.

(For an exercise pertaining to the Moon's Nodes, see Appendix II: Chapter 5: The Nodes.)

Chapter 6

Responsibility

The most commonly acknowledged astrological signature that happens in our late fifties is the Saturn Return. This also happens in our late twenties because Saturn takes approximately twenty-nine years to circle the zodiac. At this point in our journey toward elderhood we will explore what it is that Saturn offers to the process of transforming an adult into an elder.

Saturn is the farthest planet that is visible to the naked eye. The planets out past Saturn are relatively recent in human awareness.[1] Ancient sky gazers didn't necessarily know that Saturn was the farthest planet. What they knew was that it had the slowest journey through the sky. It marked a longer period of time than any of the other "wandering stars," or planets. For this reason Saturn came to be associated with all things old. In modern times "old" has become a bit of a dirty word but for ancient peoples it was connected to wisdom—the kind you can only get if you live through enough seasons. Once the outer planets began to be discovered in the eighteenth century Saturn's meaning expanded to include its close relationship to them.

Astrologically speaking the outer planets symbolize powerful trends that sweep through a culture—historic changes like the industrial revolution or the current technological revolution.

These powerful trends can easily overwhelm the lives of individuals through no fault of their own. Outer planets are called *transpersonal* planets. They represent complexes of energy that are beyond the reach of the individual self and therefore can swamp the ego. Saturn is the symbolic representative of all that protects us from the madness and disorientation that these outer planets represent. It makes sure we know the limits of the circumstantial world. As Saturn up in the sky holds the limits of what the eye, unaided by a telescope, can see so it is believed to help us hold our boundaries. Saturn doesn't care about achieving cosmic consciousness unless we do it with our feet on the ground. It is a hard taskmaster because it protects us by immersing us in circumstance. It indicates the need for real, measurable limits. If we are in rebellion or denial about these limits we may dissociate from material reality. Where Saturn is concerned this is not a reasonable response. Saturn is like the Zen master with the stick. As Jack Kornfield says, "If you tell a Zen master everything is like a dream, she will take her stick and whack you over the head. Then she will ask, "Is that a dream?" [2]

The Saturn Return is the actual moment when the planet returns to the same sign and house it was in when you were born. The first time it returned you were between twenty-seven and thirty. The second time it returns is between fifty-eight and sixty and if you are long lived it will return a third time when you are about eighty-eight. This third Saturn Return ushers in a period of life—should we be so lucky to live that long—which I have named the cycle of the *living ancestor*. By the time you achieve the realm of the living ancestors nothing is required of you externally. At this point in your life you are obviously old. You may be healthy and alert but just as a new baby comes to us from seemingly nothing so a living ancestor has one foot in this world and the other in that unknowable nothingness. A person may be more or less aware of this, may have religious beliefs about it or not, but in a sense the phase of the living ancestor is so deeply internal that the only participation required in the Great Round of existence at this stage is simply to be. To achieve that period of life with awareness, you must first master the art of being an elder.

In the human body, Saturn has rulership over bones and joints. These parts of our bodies allow us to have structure and to bend in appropriate places. Many rail against Saturn's influence when they are young because it demands discipline. In all my years of practice however I have rarely seen anyone, young or old, complain after going through a Saturn period—if they actually did what they had to do. Discipline enables mastery and we humans seem to enjoy mastering the material world.

Saturn's job is to define. A keyword sentence I learned in my early days of studying astrology is that Saturn defines *what you can do, what you can't do and what you must do*. It is this type of kitchen-table wisdom that suggests that by knowing our limits we can know where we aren't limited as well as where we might benefit from acquiring knowledge or expertise. Saturn represents the wisdom that can only come with experience.

Once upon a time we were very young. We had so little experience of the world that we didn't know that if you drop something it will fall, if you hit someone they are likely to hit you back, if you run out into the road you could be squashed and if you eat vegetables and fruit instead of sugar your teeth will have fewer cavities. We were ignorant of the ways of the world. People older than we were knew many of these things. They showed us the ropes. They played the role of Saturn for us before we could play it for ourselves. To understand our relationship to this principle we need to understand who those managers of our early lives were and how we reacted to them. (See Appendix II: Saturn: 1)

A bit about the gender of Saturn: I'm not sure if a planet (astrologically speaking) should really be assigned a gender. I'm sure in the cosmic sense every planetary symbol has a yin as well as a yang side. When astrologers think about Saturn symbolically, they refer to Saturn as "him" and rarely as "her." Saturn has been commonly associated with the father principle, father time and the grim reaper with his scythe over his shoulder waiting to cut us down.

Saturn is about limits. It is about the circumstances of being alive in a material world. For almost everyone the first person to set limits is Mom. She's our first boss. She knows the rules. She knows the system. She *is* the system. Even if Dad is the primary caregiver, fathers tend to be more permissive than mothers in the way of learning these kinds of things. They have an instinct for exploration of the world rather than containment. The way I see it is that as the Sun and Jupiter are father-related, the Moon and Saturn are generally about mother. This bears mentioning in a patriarchal world where society is still controlled and managed primarily by men, many of whom seem to be slow learners when it comes to knowing the limits of matter. (See Appendix II: Exercises: Saturn: 1.)

For the first twenty-one years of our lives the external world establishes limits for us. [3] At twenty-one with about seven years left till the return, we begin to move toward events that set the tone and circumstance of our adult experience. As we navigate through our twenties, moving all the while toward adulthood, we tend to fluctuate between doing exactly as we were conditioned to do and taking what we have been given and turning it into something of our own making.

Then comes the first Saturn Return. This moment, which lasts from about the age of twenty-seven through thirty, cracks open the shell of our childhood conditioning. We begin the long journey of turning it into some kind of expertise to be used throughout adult life. For some of us childhood is a time of being shaped and molded by people and circumstances that encourage the unfolding of life in loving, intelligent and supportive ways. For many others childhood conditioning is a time of great suffering because the adults around us are abusive or neglectful and only offer models of dysfunctional behavior. It is possible when future generations look back on the latter part of the twentieth century and the early days of the twenty-first they will consider it the Age of the Dysfunctional Family. The nuclear family may be seen as a failed experiment within which to raise healthy humans. As we come more and more to understand the meaning of *it takes a village to raise a child* our family structures are evolving. Many of us who grew up in seemingly "normal" family structures are nonetheless deeply affected by the intensity of relationship in a nuclear family.

Whatever your personal history and perspective, the more damage we experience as children the more we must transform Saturn's message. Humans learn best that which they learn by example. Saturn defines things. If our childhood was healthy and loving it is easier to simply walk the path that has been indicated. If we walk the path that is indicated by dysfunctional parents we doom ourselves to repeating the patterns of dysfunction in our own adult lives. In either case during the time of the first Saturn Return we get a good look at how it is that our childhood conditioning has set the stage for our adult life. We have the opportunity to take this information and use it in a way that will enable us to live successful adult lives, or not. (See Appendix II: Exercises: Saturn: 2.)

It is true that most of us don't consult astrologers as a matter of course at twenty-nine. We may go through this transition without the benefit of having it mapped out. Nevertheless, conscious or not, we are defining how we were brought up and what we intend to do with that upbringing through the choices we make at this time.

Although I have painted a picture of Saturn as parental, specifically mother-oriented, as a child grows and experiences the world outside the home Saturn can be any adult figure that sets limits. It can also be found in the social environment that contains the family as it too will restrict and define the world that we experience. Growing up in a war zone defines one reality while growing up where there has never been a war defines a completely different reality.

One of the amazing things about the social environment of the late twentieth and early twenty-first centuries is the availability of virtual realities. Our group of elders has largely grown up with escapism as an accepted way of dealing with how we live. There have always been alcohol, drugs and entertainment but the world at this moment gives us the opportunity to live virtually in an exceptionally stunning way. When we have had enough of reality we all know where to go. We even can use spirituality and psychology to avoid living in the real world of form. Saturn represents the fact that sooner or later the piper will require payment. There are consequences to all our actions. This simple, basic truth is the cornerstone of responsibility. If we do not have the *ability to respond* to the manifest world we will not be successful. By cultivating our ability to respond we empower ourselves to engage with life as if we have at least helped to create it. The most unconscious thing to do as an elder is to respond to age as if someone is doing it to you; as if someone knows more about you than you do; as if there is some authority that has the last word. Our response to authority really shows up as we approach the end of our lives and become more dependent on others for our well being.

For Esther her late twenties were a time when she and her husband lived in a foreign country for his work. This disconnected her from her musical world. For a while she taught piano but by the age of thirty had stopped. Shortly after that she became ill. Thus began the major task of her adult life which was educating herself and ultimately others on the powerful connection between the mind and the body. She went to 'school' in a sense inspired by the realization that somehow her illness was about the fact that she was not living the life she felt called to live. Without her music she became ill. On one hand it was terrible to suddenly have to deal with a life threatening illness. On the other she was totally grateful to encounter the world of alternative medicine and the work of bringing the body, mind and emotions into a harmony with each other.

For Linda this period marked the beginning of her career. She was offered a management position but had to hold back because her children were young and she felt that her responsibilities lay in caring for them. Looking back she realizes that by staying home with her children in those early years she became vividly aware of society's need for healing. As a mother she began to see that this healing would be most effective if it dealt with the needs of individuals as members of society. From this she ultimately chose her career as a social worker.

When Kate was in her late twenties she was already married and well placed in her corporate life. She and her husband were planning for their first child and looking at how to manage a family as well as their careers. Kate wanted it all and believed that she could have it if she just managed it well.

The second Saturn Return at around the age of fifty-eight is, astrologically speaking, the official end of adult life and the beginning of life as an elder. In North America we are generally not considered to be senior citizens until the age of sixty-five. Becoming an elder is not the same as being a senior citizen although it's clearly related. There is no age for mandatory retirement or special discounts in the symbolic realm.

What was so hard for our mothers about this transition and is still a challenge for many people at this age today is that our culture doesn't generally honor the passage that takes us from smooth and innocent to wrinkly and potentially wise. But we need not despair. The very act of sitting here and reading this kind of book is a genuine attempt at changing this.

We are bombarded with the distorted belief that aging is a sickness and only drugs and surgery will help us to see it through. The arsenal against aging includes ERT, Viagra, Botox, not to mention the overwhelming array of health food supplements including herbs and vitamins that we have to choose from if we can sort out the information. It behooves a consumer driven economy to keep us from seeing elderhood as a normal, healthy part of life. As the world goes through its extreme changes our efforts at envisioning and creating a new and healthy image of what it means to be an elder is a very important and empowering thing to do. We change the world when we change ourselves. Because we are people of great privilege in Western society we can make the mistake of not valuing the part each individual—including ourselves—plays in potentially changing the world. As privileged beings we accept the status quo more readily even when it doesn't serve us. It is quite revolutionary to retrieve a lost piece of an archetype and consciously express it in ways that we can recognize as authentic reflections of our true nature. Even as I write this I see things changing. Kate remembers her grandmother's involvement in her small community in an effort to preserve the green space in her town, which was already suffering from encroachment by developers. When she thinks of the passion and focus her grandmother brought to this task she is inspired to look forward to her own elder years.

One of Saturn's major messages is about responsibility. Above and beyond the traditional meaning of responsibility, think of this as the ability to respond. During our first Saturn cycle, other people are responsible for us. We respond to their commands, their rules and the limits they set for us. We learn a tremendous amount about what will be expected of us as humans by watching how the adults in our lives take responsibility for us. Simple psychology tells us that if your mother neglected you, you may grow up to neglect your own children, marry someone who neglects them or just fear you are doing it even if you're not. If your mother was present and loving, you will grow up expecting that this is how mothers are meant to handle children. Clearly there are people who were neglected as children who figure out how to be responsible parents and people from good homes who abdicate responsibility, but in either case they are still reacting to what they observed and experienced in their own childhood.

During the middle cycle we are responsible for others. In the past men and women generally approached this in different ways, which were determined by society. For the generations using this book, we know that the expectations we started out with as we entered adulthood—expectations about families and careers—have changed even as we have been living them. For many of us as children the expectation of a "typical" home was that Mom stayed home with the kids and Dad earned the money to support the family. Many of us grew up that way and many of us didn't, but it was still considered the optimal family situation. Since the 1960s these roles have gradually fallen by the wayside.

Many mothers are both nurturers and wage earners for their families. Stay-at-home-dad is a relatively new term. There have always been dead-beat dads who abandoned their families—even mothers have been known to abandon their families—and these tragic abdications of responsibility seem to have proliferated over the last third of the twentieth century.

Although this is sad and wreaks havoc in the lives of individuals and communities, it may be the necessary fallout during a time of transformation from the old to the new. One of the greatest and possibly most controversial gains for women in Western Society is the right to divorce which goes hand in hand with the right to choose to marry or not. No longer are women officially ostracized for their choices around marriage. Although we may not be aware of this as we make our own choices it does ultimately affect the structure of society. Most likely it takes a few generations to integrate such a change into the social fabric. This is a good example of how change may bring chaos but ultimately it will offer a new and preferable way of functioning. We think of *choice* as the right to choose to have children or not but although the laws are in place it will take some time for men and women to get used to the fact that married is not the only way in which a woman can find enough security for herself and her children.

Some of us take on our adult responsibility at an emotional level. We support people who are dependent upon us through caring for them psychologically. Others may express their sense of responsibility more in terms of offering material support. During the middle cycle of Saturn in our adult years we respond to the needs of others; whether or not we realize it, we are responding to the status quo by trying to uphold or escape from it.

If you truly want to change society in your adult years the tendency will be to do it from within the system. Generally it is people under the age of twenty-nine who have the impulse and the freedom to be truly revolutionary. They have less responsibility and therefore less to lose. Perhaps it is also true that people over sixty—the elders—who are finished with building and supporting the world can work significantly toward changing the system.

What they have that the 20 year olds do not is a lot of insight as to what does and doesn't work based on their experience.

One of the interesting things about Saturn is that although we generally think of it as the planet of responsibility it is also the planet that reveals itself in some people as the impulse to escape from responsibility. As an example of this, let's say there are two people and they each have children. One person works hard to the best of their ability and provides those children with all they will need to grow into healthy adults. The other neglects the children and falls into some kind of addictive behavior. Each of our examples is responding to the call of responsibility. One responds by picking up the task and the other runs from it, but both are responding to it. During the adult years, whether you do what is expected of you or you run as far as you can from it, you are undoubtedly reacting to responsibility's call.

As we move into Saturn's third cycle as elders we begin to want to cultivate the ability to respond to *ourselves.* We are tired of saying what we don't want to say, doing what we don't want to do. This is a time when we are pretty sure we have done our part. We know that even for the benefit of our adult (or soon to be adult) children, it is healthier to respond to our own needs. Some of us are so out of the habit it can feel like being the new student at the University of Life taking the course Responsibility to Myself: 101.

In a book by Natalie Angiers called *Women: An Intimate Geography,* I came across a discussion of the Grandmother Hypothesis, [4] which seems relevant to consider as we talk of Saturn in the elder years. The Grandmother Hypothesis states that menopause and the female post-reproductive life span evolved in humans because it greatly benefits the survival of the species. Ceasing reproduction when the likelihood of death during childbirth reached a certain threshold and concentrating resources on helping daughters reproduce far outweighed the advantages of continued childbirth.

This theory has been around since the 1950s. Apparently it applies only to maternal grandmothers. It appears that back in the day although men hunted they didn't contribute much to the day-to-day gathering that sustained life. Meat was more about position and power. The grandmothers could help by gathering enough to feed more than one or even two people because they were unencumbered with children.

Clearly this theory describes one of the significant contributions women have made to the evolution of the human race. This input from the grandmothers would have benefited both men and women because it benefited the entire group. When the human race was in its early stages of evolution that use was to help support the mothers and children so that as a species we could multiply. I am sure that this hypothesis is still significant. If the human race makes it through the alarming transformation of the moment it will be, at least in part, because of elders (both men and women this time) and their concern for their children and their children's children. It's quite possible that the Grandmother Hypothesis is as relevant today as it has ever been.

I don't believe that the impulse to be more authentically ourselves, to speak truth, to respond to who we are is about being selfish. Some may interpret it that way, as if being an elder is permission to be narcissistic. But mostly this impulse toward greater authenticity is driven by an instinct about which we have very little understanding or appreciation. As our days of estrogen-style care-giving and testosterone-driven wage-earning come to an end, we need to listen deep within ourselves to figure out what is next. There is no road map at the moment, although there are many clues. Of course we will need this skill of responding to our inner being as we get older and older because as we get weaker in old age it is this ability to respond to ourselves that will allow us to meet death with equanimity. Along the way, however, it is possible that the ability to shift toward hearing the still, small voice of inner truth will be the contribution we make to our evolving species. It is a shift we make not just for ourselves but for all sentient beings.

One of my favorite evolutionary theories is that the human race as a whole is still in an adolescent phase. [5] This occurred to me when my daughter was a teenager. The incredible changes in the body and brain of an adolescent and the behavior that occurs in response to these changes are frightening to behold at times. Sexual obsession, greed, violence, self-centeredness, lack of compassion—traits common among teenagers—are also common in society as a whole.

In a book called *The Sibling Society,* [6] Robert Bly speaks of adolescents and adults and what is required of the adults. I believe what he is saying applies to the role of elders as well:

> What is asked of adults now is that they stop going forward, to retirement, to Costa Rica, to fortune, and turn to face the young siblings (humans) and the adolescents. One can imagine a field with the adolescents on one side of a line drawn on the earth and adults on the other side looking into their eyes. The adult in our time is asked to reach his or her hand across the line and pull the youth into adulthood. . . . The hope lies in the longing we have to be adults. If we take an interest in younger ones . . . then our own feeling of being adult will be augmented, and adulthood might again appear to be a desirable state for many young ones.

I think that Bly is touching on a core issue that Saturn brings. If we think of the entire society as adolescent, not just the teenagers, we can imagine he is speaking of all those who cannot make it across the line from childhood into adulthood and then elderhood. We are living in a time when the entire world seems like one miserable adolescent! There is very little to inspire us to grow up. As elders, one of our responsibilities is to create an image of our stage of life that allows those younger than us to be interested in what we think and who we are. In this way they will see it as a part of their lives to come. If, when we are young, we have an image of ourselves as living into an interesting and healthy old age, we might be less fearful of aging.

Our culture encourages us to stay young forever, to be young even when we are old. It's a bad idea. It is good sense to stay healthy till we die but not young. For one thing it's a whole lot of unnecessary and pointless effort, but more importantly it makes it very difficult for others to desire to grow older.

What we haven't quite defined yet is how the responsibilities of an adult are different from those of an elder. Even if we understand the value of defining the elder years as distinct from the adult years we aren't sure how this is done. Of course there is no general prescription that works for everyone. To do this takes a certain amount of reflection. We might look back to our childhood and see how the conditioning we experienced then led us to our adult choices. Then we would need to imagine how that could play itself out from the perspective of elderhood. (See Appendix II: Saturn exercises)

When I was in my late fifties I had the opportunity to take a road trip to the Arctic. I had always dreamed of being north of the Arctic Circle and experiencing the midnight sun. As I traveled with my companion along the highways and byways of this delicate ecosystem I couldn't help but notice the large numbers of elders traveling this route in their RVs. At first I was horrified by the size of the vehicles and the old guys at the wheel. Not only were they guzzling gas at an alarming rate, carrying only two people per vehicle, but they also seemed to be a danger on the road. It was like some strange cultural pocket of rampant individualism and consumption. A debate between me and my friend broke out. He saw what they were doing as the ultimate freedom; I saw it as the ultimate unconsciousness. I decided to consider it from my habitual symbolic perspective—no judgments, just observation and interpretation.

Here is what I observed through personal encounters with the RV-ers as well as watching them from a distance: A large number of elders on the road, seemingly ignorant of the footprint of their means of travel, are eager for experience and blessed with a sense of entitlement. The feeling that they were tourists in this world rather than pilgrims struck me over and over. Tourists live outside the world they move through, pilgrims are one with the experience and learn from everything in a desire to grow in awareness. The hunger of the RV-ers for the next great site and the communication network among fellow travelers of bragging and anticipating it were strong. The more I observed the more I had to acknowledge that, although we were not traveling in an RV or part of that particular pocket of culture, our motivation for traveling through the Arctic wasn't much different. We had always wanted to go and so we did. It might be our last chance for such a trip. I was humbled and fascinated by the fact that this entitlement that was so obvious in others was also at work in me. That was as objective as I could get.

Questions arose in me. Why would elders be so unaware of their heavy footprint in a time of such pervasive awareness of impending ecological disaster? Maybe the fierce individualist cowboy mentality of North Americans is at work here. Clearly it is an extension of the culture at large and not specific to elders.

Maybe the reason that so many elders are taking to the road in their RVs is because they have no road map, no inner direction. In some way they are condemned to travel via the external road map, never knowing why they travel and never reaching a goal because there isn't any. Elders with no sense of the meaning of elderhood could easily give themselves over to excessive consumption, demanding, even claiming their *reward* because there is no sense of the inherent value of this stage of life. The notion that this empty wandering could be my reward made me want to howl with anxiety. My deep sense is that there are no external rewards for becoming an elder. It's just what happens to us if we are lucky. We don't deserve what we get, we simply and profoundly create our elderhood based on how we have lived up to this point. But surely, without an inner map it is impossible to find meaning in the outer one. I never found it possible to have this discussion with the elders I met on the road because it was too challenging.

But I did talk to women I met in Laundromats, restaurants or at interesting sites about their children and husbands, the homes that they missed and often a sense of the accomplishments or lack thereof that they carried with them.

Esther's reflection on this topic leads her to muse that as a child she was burdened with guilt. She felt that everything was her fault. As an adult she worked hard to alleviate suffering in herself primarily and then in others. As an elder she is struck by the way that suffering permeates all lives in some way. She has come to understand that there is much meaning in suffering.

Linda says she felt burdened as a child by the expectation that somehow she was meant to take care of things the adults could not. As an adult she took on many responsibilities and did more than her share. As a baby elder she is working hard to come to terms with what it means to be truly responsive and therefore responsible to herself without letting other people down. It's a rocky road so far.

Kate reflects that her childhood was a time when people expected her to be excellent. She didn't mind this as it felt that she wanted it as well. She is interested in the notion that she may have to tease out her own sense of excellence from that of her parents to experience a meaningful elder period in her life. At this point in her anticipation of elderhood she can only marvel that this will somehow come to her. Turning inward has not been her way. She is curious about the fact that introspection may be something that is required in the natural order of things as one grows older.

Many people are born when their parents are in their late twenties at the threshold of their adult lives. Many of us had our children at this stage of our lives. These are particularly interesting markers because having a child at this time of life is an indication that the child is the embodiment of the adult's responsibilities. You and your child will go through these major stage changes at the same time. The parent will become elder as the child becomes adult. It is worth contemplating how our parents might have been faring when they were the age we are now. (Appendix II: Exercises: Saturn)

Of all the astrological signposts we have looked at so far Saturn is the one that generally presents us with the greatest challenge because it is about the earthly manifestation of our circumstances. You have had your children, you have made your fortune, you have acquired your physical strengths and weaknesses. You can embellish these or not but you exist in a certain container and you must work with it.

In the larger culture in which we all live, the Saturn principle has been estranged from its core meaning. It has been dressed in the trappings of the bottom line of the corporate world. Saturn's inherent gift is the wisdom that can only come through experience and the commitment to use that wisdom as a resource for the good of all. This has been twisted by greed and domination into a shape virtually the opposite of the principle it actually represents.

As women our accomplishments have traditionally been marginalized. We are taught that if we want recognition from the larger culture we must be like men. Those women born from the late 1930s on are the first generation to be up front about seeing their accomplishments through the eyes of one another. This is radical. As women who have accomplished this feat of self-awareness in our adult lives we must now tackle the issue of the marginalizing of elders—especially female elders. At this stage we do not need to be the star of the show nor should we sit back as though we have nothing to offer, no purpose to fulfill as elders. As elders we aspire to find a balance between those things that make us unique as individuals and the awareness that we are a kind of focus point in the great stream of humanity that connects to our ancestors and to those who will come after us.

It can be difficult to engage with these issues. They are often hard to name because many of us feel so inadequate anyway. Here you stand. Your adult life is done but you live in a world that offers no image for the next stage, aside from how consuming this drug or that vacation experience will make you vital and young (again). You instinctively know that trying to stay young will be another version of the rat race, but becoming old in the tradition of your mother seems at best outmoded and at worst terrifying. The time has come to clean out the closet of outworn images and create some new ones. To do this we must first consider our regrets. (See Appendix II: Exercises: Saturn.)

Regrets are not the same as failures. As Bob Dylan says, there is "no success like failure and failure's no success at all."[7] Even so, there are things we just couldn't or didn't do. Often it's the things we couldn't accomplish that shape and mold us. We need to look them in the eye to come of age. We need to see what we have learned—and to accept how these things have contributed to making us the person we are at this moment. Such is the nature of life.

It is common for younger people to blame older people for the conditions they inherit both personally and globally. We did it when we were young. As we transition into our elder years it does not make sense to take the blame as a generation for a species on the verge of extinction due to our own behavior. One of the most horrifying and liberating revelations of elder life is that no one is to blame yet we are all responsible for our actions. Human beings are so easily conditioned to behave the way they do. Ignorance of who we are and what makes us tick is a given. Generally the regrets we encounter as we enter the realm of our elderhood can be boiled down to this: We did the best we could with what we had and sometimes (not always) it seems that it just wasn't good enough (for us as we look back).

People will tell you that regret is a useless emotion, and certainly it is pointless to live there. But understanding our personal and universal feelings of regret ultimately softens our hearts and allows us a greater humility and acceptance of the human condition.

Esther's deepest regret is that she spent so much time enraged about things she could not control that it ultimately made her ill. Looking back she realizes that she was endlessly shamed and angry that her parents preferred their son to their daughter. She regrets that she felt this same thing from her husband—that he preferred his work to his life with her. The sadness is in the fact that letting it enrage her was a choice she made. She could possibly have chosen to feel the feelings of her sorrow rather than project them onto her husband and her life. Having learned that the physiological state of rage is the same as that of anxiety she regrets that she didn't simply deal with how anxious she was with the feeling that she was not lovable.

Linda regrets that she spent so much of her life feeling that she wasn't doing enough. She sees that the shame and fear she felt around her father's alcoholism translated to a feeling that she must make up for how awful this world is—especially to its children. She deeply regrets her choice of a partner and father to her children. She also has regret about how this constellation of behavior meant that she experienced very little joy even as she became an accomplished person in the world.

For Kate the experience of reflecting on her deepest regrets has not yet arrived. What she is aware of however is a sense of regret that grew in her mother as she entered her 60s. She seemed wistful and inattentive and when asked what was troubling her she had no answer. One day before Kate's first child was born she and her mother were having lunch after shopping for baby things. Totally out of the blue her mother began to speak of a deep love she had for a man she met when she was young. He came from a different background and there was no way they could marry. Her eyes filled with tears and she confessed that although she has always dearly loved her husband she has never forgotten this other love. Kate was truly moved by this sharing and instinctively understood that somehow she was required to offer her mother some kind of forgiveness. The memory of this day faded from Kate's mind as time passed but in looking at this exercise she remembers how touched she was.

As we approach elderhood, we need to look at the accomplishments of our adult lives. These may or may not be the things recognized as achievements in the world. They are the things that fill you with the feeling of success or satisfaction.

They may be one-time events, such as the time you sold the most or won the contest or figured out how to make something. They may be moments when your heart was open, when you helped someone in need. They may be accomplishments that took your whole life (thus far) to achieve, such as forgiving one of your parents, quitting smoking or drinking, raising a well-adjusted child, or fostering a long-lasting marriage.

Accomplishments may seem easier to reflect upon than our regrets. For many of us there is a *yes, but* feeling that accompanies our sense of accomplishment. And there is also the natural defensiveness that says, *Well, I don't want to reflect on my accomplishments because I'm not done yet.* Indeed, reviewing our accomplishments at this stage of life is not about being done or even about shoring up our self-esteem. It's about weighing the relative value of success. As we become elders we are meant to reorient our lives to reflect the maturation of our values. Often the value of success in adult life comes from others recognizing what we have done. As elders this may not feel as satisfying as it once was. By reviewing our accomplishments we are also teasing out a sense of how our values are changing.

Esther recognizes that over time her successes have become more internal. She started out wanting to be the smartest and now she is able to gain deep satisfaction when she has moments of quiet wisdom. She is totally aware that although she has deep regrets about her rage she has gained an immense amount of wisdom from the journey of self healing.

Linda feels accomplished in all that she has learned from the people she has worked with as well as the knowledge she has of herself. Although she is regretful of her choice of a mate she is proud and feels accomplished that she has raised relatively healthy children who plan to make a contribution to this world. She is proud that, hard as it has been, she has made life better for more than a few people and even on a bad day she shows up for her life as required.

Kate can list many of her accomplishments on her resume. She suspects that as she truly enters the realm of her elder years these will not be the accomplishments that she will be most proud of.

As we develop an elder perspective on the regrets and ambitions of our adult lives we can then begin to imagine the road ahead with the same elder perspective. Looking down that road we begin to understand that the measure of our success or happiness isn't about getting it right or even getting others to think we got it right. Possibly the only measure of our success will be found in how totally we can live into the present moment with all our human failings and wondrous abilities.

As elders it is a truly radical act to know deep inside ourselves that we have the strength and wisdom to cultivate the ability to respond from within ourselves over and above the demands from the outer structure. It inevitably gives rise to a sense of gentle empowerment around what it is that we can actually accomplish in the elder phase of life.

LOVE AND RESPONSIBILITY

In the last chapter—the Love Affair—we talked about the Moon. The Moon is the container for our feelings and the heavenly body that symbolizes our ability to bond and get our needs met. Saturn is the opposite principle. Saturn calls us to look, not at comfort and security but at discipline and responsibility.

Astrologically, as mentioned above, there is a special relationship between the Moon and Saturn. It can be seen in a few different ways. One is that they rule opposite signs. The Moon rules Cancer, the first sign of summer and Saturn rules Capricorn, the first sign of winter. Rulership is an important concept in the language of astrology. A planet is like a king or a queen, and it is said to have an affinity for a sign, which is akin to a country over which it rules. Cancer and Capricorn are signs that are opposite each other in the wheel of the year as winter and summer are opposite one another. Oppositions are about challenge. One side of the opposition shows the other side what it's made of. In the dead of winter we remember summer and the contrast helps us to deal with the circumstances of winter. Winter requires a lot of discipline (we all remember our mothers telling us to bundle up against the cold). Summer is a time of abundance of food, more social contact and greater ease.

The other thing that is significant is that Saturn takes about twenty-nine years to go around the zodiac once and the Moon takes about twenty-nine days. Astrological thought, symbolic thought, often works with the notion of correspondences. "As above, so below" is the universal tenet of astrology. When you look at the world through the lens of symbolism the power that drives it is in being able to link things together. That is, we see mostly through reflection. In astrology then, it is perfectly sensible to make a day equal a year. [8] We then can say that by progression (one day equals one year) the Moon moves at the same speed as Saturn. This is a very strong affinity in the world of symbolic thinking.

The Moon as a symbol of comfort and security would be very weak if it wasn't contained in a strong vessel. We all know of the ineffectuality of parents who love their children but don't teach them the skills they need to succeed in the world so they can fulfill their potential. Saturn as a symbol of structure and discipline would be dry and brittle without the watery light of the Moon to infuse it with feeling and therefore meaning.

The poetic sensibility we explored in Chapter 5 and the question of authority we investigated in this chapter are the front and the back of each other. For any relationship to thrive, even the one between your soul and your body, there needs to be a strong container within which to hold it. However you go about accomplishing this task it is worth the time and the effort to give birth to the notion of elderhood because by creating a new image we contribute significantly to the need of our species to transform the cultural stereotypes of the throwaway mentality. We know that it is good for the planet to reduce, reuse and recycle, and as we are a valuable human resource we need to apply the same principles to our own lives. There is no doubt that as elders we can practice the "three Rs": we can reduce our consumption as everyone should but on a different level we can reuse and recycle our experience that we may find meaning in our life. By so doing we offer to those who come after the possibility of finding meaning in their lives. We are ancestors in the making, and we will leave the clues for those that follow. Not because of our worldly success or failures but because we learned from our experience. We valued that learning and we lived by our ability to bear or suffer what we learned. It is perhaps our suffering that is the greatest gift if we can find meaning in it. As Helen M. Luke says:

> Every time a person exchanges neurotic depression for real suffering, he or she is sharing to some small degree in the carrying of the suffering of mankind, in bearing a tiny part of the darkness of the world. Such a one is released from his small personal concern into a sense of *meaning.* One may not be consciously thinking in those terms, but the transition can immediately be recognized by the disappearance of the frustrated pointlessness of mood and depression. It is as though we become aware of a new dimension. Meaning has entered the experience. [9]

(For an exercises pertaining to Saturn, see Appendix II: Chapter 6: Saturn.)

Chapter 7

Threshold: Chaos, Crisis, Change

Here we have come to the end of the beginning. From the perspective of becoming and being elders we have explored our hearts desire, our basic emotional programming, how we defend our lives with our personality, our basic relationship qualities, the body/soul relationship, our karmic task, our fundamental beliefs and our responsibility factor. We are prepared in the best way possible; we have the right questions.

At this point in our exploration of elderhood we have some understanding of the three stages of life and some enthusiasm for embracing the third stage. It is as the poet William Blake said, there is innocence akin to ignorance, there is experience—a sometimes obscure and difficult teacher—and there is higher innocence, which can only arise as experience removes the scales of ignorance from our eyes. In our exploration of Saturn we encountered the notion of limits and the sense that these limits teach us about the world we live in. Sometimes they are cruel and unfortunate. Other times they are well meant and educational. In any case we learn to navigate the world based on our experience of these limits. We learn discipline of one sort or another and hopefully we become wiser. This wisdom that can only come with experience opens the door to our higher innocence.

Now we are ready to look at the actual nature of the threshold. What is this imaginary line we are crossing that will enable us to leave our adult selves and become elders? As we step from one reality into another we must relinquish something familiar for something unknown. The very nature of a threshold gives rise to a certain amount of chaos and crises which ultimately leads us to change. The actual moment of crossing a threshold requires a tremendous amount of courage if we are to remain awake and aware in the transition. We must have courage to overcome our fear of the unknown because we have no choice but to move into it. Instinctively we fear the letting go that this elder threshold requires because we are used to believing that our world holds together based on the controls we use to keep it that way. What we need to learn as elders especially and what the new science of chaos theory suggests is that it is quite possible that there is an underlying order to the universe. Too much control blocks the quantum leap that might create a new level of order which could actually be an improvement.

As Bernadette Brady says in her book *Astrology: A Place in Chaos:*

> The source of new order is not causal and logical but rather it spontaneously emerges from the void. Order is not created by an artisan entity thinking about what to design today but rather is a natural expression of a relationship-rich, womb-like void. [1]

Keeping too tight a hold on the order we have created in our adult lives necessitates a lack of awareness and a strong dose of denial. This may actually make things worse. We become brittle and likely to break apart. Of course if this happens we ultimately come to chaos in an unwilling frame of mind which is just that much more difficult. I suspect that by embracing chaos in a conscious way we can move through it with more grace and less panic.

Since the dawn of our human perception of time, brought on no doubt by the inevitability of death, humans have had to live with the awareness of the unraveling of order which comes at the end of everything. We seem to be the only animal with a conscious awareness of our aging and ultimate death. We have been stalked more or less by the fear of falling apart as we age. The alternative (to die young) is definitely not more appealing for most of us, however.

When humans are faced with fear of chaos they naturally want to create order. As infants and young children our bodies and minds are chaotic to begin with. We don't know how to use them well. We depended on our parents to create external rhythms to hold us in place until we learned the trick of holding ourselves together. As adults we held the world together as best we could for ourselves and those who were dependent upon us. As elders we are faced once again with a sense of varying levels of inner instability on the physical as well as mental and emotional levels. We do our best to create and maintain rhythms to keep us healthy but we become increasingly aware that today's ache and pain could be tomorrow's condition. At this time of our lives, unlike infancy and childhood, however, we are aware of the difference between inner and outer realities. We have the option of perspective.

Something that I believe is a unique experience for elders of the twentieth and twenty-first centuries is how the external world seems to be more chaotic and crises laden than ever. We are aware of the world in its global totality in a way we were not before and as time goes on it seems to descend more and more into crises and chaos. This awareness of the world falling apart has been brilliantly articulated by the poet William Butler Yeats in a much-quoted poem written in 1919 just after the end of the First World War. This war to end all wars brought us into a period of chaos which continues still. Although this poem is well known in parts I am offering it here in its entirety because of its visionary eloquence.

"THE SECOND COMING"

by William Butler Yeats

Turning and turning in the widening gyre
The falcon cannot hear the falconer;
Things fall apart; the centre cannot hold;
Mere anarchy is loosed upon the world,
The blood-dimmed tide is loosed, and everywhere
The ceremony of innocence is drowned;
The best lack all conviction, while the worst
Are full of passionate intensity.

Surely some revelation is at hand;
Surely the Second Coming is at hand.
The Second Coming! Hardly are those words out
When a vast image out of *Spiritus Mundi*
Troubles my sight: somewhere in sands of the desert
A shape with lion body and the head of a man,
A gaze blank and pitiless as the sun,
Is moving its slow thighs, while all about it
Reel shadows of the indignant desert birds.
The darkness drops again; but now I know
That twenty centuries of stony sleep
Were vexed to nightmare by a rocking cradle,
And what rough beast, its hour come round at last,
Slouches towards Bethlehem to be born?

I do not think anyone has better expressed this sense of chaos into which this world has come. The world in a global sense seems to be falling apart at a faster and faster rate at the very same time as we are entering a stage in our own process of aging that may seem the same. We have mirrors for dissolution and death everywhere.

When we look out into the world beyond our own personal garden gate in which we are becoming elders it does not reflect a peaceful ordered container within which we can grow old. It is by no means relaxing to contemplate the world which our precious grandchildren will inherit. What we see reflected is a chaotic transformation whose only promise seems to be that nothing will ever be the same again.

Fear is one obvious response to this. Denial is another. A third possibility is to jump right in and embrace both the inner and outer world even as we cannot predict what will happen next. What we need is Prometheus.

Back in Chapter 1 we discussed the astrological events that occur in our early 50s. At that time I mentioned Richard Tarnas' discussion of how the planet Uranus might be associated with the qualities of Prometheus. With a kind of symbolic symmetry it seems fitting that one of the first aspects you encounter as you enter the decade of transition in your early 50s would be echoed in one of the last aspects which occurs at around the age of 61. In your early 50s Uranus made a soft or empowering aspect to the place where it was when you were born. Its contribution was to help us empower our intellect. At the end of that same decade Uranus makes a hard or stressful aspect to its natal position in your chart. What this seems to indicate is that what we need to face the chaos and crises of the moment is the ability to take on the system, to defy our fear and to create a revolution of consciousness in each and every one of us as individuals. We must call on the Promethean trait of fearless empowerment to make the final entry into our elder years.

The nature of Uranus is to reveal a truer perspective of reality and awaken consciousness whether you think you are ready or not. Uranus encourages us to think outside the box no matter how outside the box we already thought we were. When Uranus comes with a challenge, as it does at the beginning of our 7th decade of life, the wild and chaotic qualities of its nature are emphasized.

A little background about this planet might be interesting. When a new planet is discovered astrologers figure out what it means by looking at the events of the time period in which it was discovered. Uranus was discovered in 1781 by William and Caroline Herschel. This was a very exciting time during which the world was forever changed. It was around the time of the American and French revolutions; the beginning of the Industrial Revolution; when Ben Franklin was out there with his kite figuring out how to harness electricity. Uranus was the first of the outer planets, which cannot be seen with the naked eye, to be discovered. Of course this discovery would not have been possible without advances in technology that allowed for more powerful telescopes. Imagine that for untold ages before Uranus was discovered there were only the Sun, Moon and five planets. The way many astrologers understand the discovery of a new planet is that it is the opening of a new consciousness for humanity in general. This discovery of the first outer planet, which was invisible since the dawn of human awareness, symbolizes the beginning of nothing less than a revolution in consciousness which is reflected in the way that we live.

One of the most difficult things about this revolutionary new energy that swept through the world and continues to do so in present day society is that it changed everything including the primary relationships that hold society together. This has been hard on the elders. As Zalman Schachter-Shalomi says in his book on aging:

> Throughout most of history, elders occupied honored roles in society as sages and seers, leaders and judges, guardians of the traditions, and instructors of the young. They were revered as gurus, shamans, wise old women and men who helped guide the social order and who initiated spiritual seekers into the mysteries of inner space. Beginning with the Industrial Revolution, with its emphasis on technological knowledge that often was beyond their ken, elders lost their esteemed place in society and fell into the disempowered state that we now ascribe to a 'normal' old age.[2]

Because the outer planets have longer orbits around the Sun they appear from the perspective of earth to move more slowly through the zodiac. On account of this they are associated with sweeping changes that characterize whole generations at a time. When we are under their influence we often feel that life is happening to us rather than that we have created the situations or feelings we are having. We can be easily swept along by the times. Whether positive or negative the ego often feels overwhelmed and in awe or terrified when outer planet transits arise.

Uranus takes 84 years to make one complete cycle around the zodiac. It takes about 7 years for Uranus to transit though a sign. What this means is that each group of people born in a particular 7-year period will have Uranus in the same sign and they will be challenged in similar ways by the aspect that Uranus makes at 60.

If you were born between 1926 and 1933 (for exact dates refer to Appendix I), you have Uranus in Aries. When Uranus came to challenge you at 60 it was in the sign of Capricorn. In Aries Uranus suggests a group of people who had to be very independent to break away from the ideals of their childhood. You were born at a time of worldwide depression. People who were children then had a kind of instinctive independent streak which allowed them to think beyond the circumstances of the moment. It is interesting to note that as Uranus has an 84 year return cycle it will enter Aries again over the period of 2010 and 2011 and stay there for seven years. Once again we seem to be entering a time of great recession or depression and the children born during this period will need that same gift of independence as their great or grandparents did.

At around the age of 60, Uranus in Capricorn challenged this group of people with questions such as, "What use has all this individuality served? Who am I anyway?" As this astrological event happened between 1984 and 1998 the world began to embrace the notion that we were experiencing and would continue to experience an ecological crises of great proportion. This crisis would stir the memory of the crises of the Great Depression. As young elders at that time the challenge was to grapple with how your experience as an individual would have any relevance in the world. The need to not to be swept aside simply because you are old would be passionate among people with Uranus in Aries. Independent and possibly heroic action would be required here to keep the individual from being swallowed up in the crises of the moment even as it was when you were children.

If you were born between 1933 and 1941 you have Uranus in Taurus. This group was born during the build-up and explosion of the Second World War. The Depression was still a major factor. Change would have to come from somewhere. Taurus is a sign that speaks of values and comfort. In their 20s this group built up an image of 'the good life' that was different from what they grew up with. When Uranus came to the challenge between 1995 and 2003 it was in the sign of Aquarius—a sign of high idealism and strong collective energies. The challenge here is how to make a dream come true. This group would strive hard to create the most comfortable old age as possible. It appears that, just as many of them are settling into their comfortable old age the construct they have built is threatened by the global economic crises. As pensions and retirement funds are no longer supported by the overall economy this group may have to revise their dream and build a new one. A volatile and unpredictable stock market combined with world events makes none of us feel safe. This challenge requires an even larger commitment to unpredictability at a time when the body is getting creaky and external comfort seems to be the least you should be able to expect.

If you were born between 1942 and 1948 you have Uranus in Gemini. Uranus in Gemini is essentially clever and atypical. This is a group of people determined not to think the way their parents thought. Uranus in Gemini is challenged around the age of 60 via the sign of Pisces. If Gemini is the mind of the individual, fascinated by each and every one of the ten thousand things, Pisces signifies the universal mind which contains everything as one. The challenge for this group comes from an overload of information. No matter how clever you are, no matter how you have lived by your wits, no matter how you pride yourself on your superior intelligence, the sheer volume of information about any subject is overwhelming. Whether you are interested or involved in health, social issues, hobbies or sports there is an embarrassment of riches when it comes to information about your chosen topic. This group steps across the threshold of their elder years faced with the challenge of mental stress. You can't tune it out (because you have Uranus in Gemini) and you can't totally take it on (because you are not a fully realized being). Again, there is an internal shift that must be made—a shift in the way you use your mind. How you think (Gemini) and what you turn your mind toward when thinking becomes an issue which Uranus stirs up at around the age of sixty.

If you were born between 1948 and 1956 you have Uranus in Cancer. In their 20s this group found many ways to run away from home. Many of them literally did become runaways but many others set their sails toward an ideal that said they would not live in the chaos of the apparent destruction of the nuclear family. This group knows the truth that it takes a village to keep a family healthy. As they began to come of age they were open to experiments in living. This group will experience the challenge to their Uranus from the sign of Aries. Their challenge will be about living as elders in a world that is transforming radically and becoming a bit like the Wild West. At a time in life when they want nothing more than to be held in the secure support of community they will have the opportunity to put their minds to work helping to solve the problem of transforming society from the chaos of the disintegrating nuclear family into a way to live together in communities. As this group become elders it may well be necessary for elders to live with their children's families if everyone's needs are to be met. Perhaps the notion of homes for the aged will give way to communities that include young and old alike.

Uranus is often an indicator of hyper mental energy when it presents a challenge. Therefore around the age of sixty it is easy for anyone to feel mentally over stimulated. Becoming elders in the information age only intensifies the experience. Often, when a client is under the influence of Uranus the best thing the astrologer can say is, "Expect the unexpected!" When Uranus shows its face in your life you know that you are stepping off some kind of edge and you will never be the same. You are leaving the known world behind. What an apt image for the uncharted territory of being an elder in this world of ours.

If you think of Uranus's eighty-four-year cycle, then at sixty it has traveled three quarters of the way around. The first time it challenged you was in your early twenties. If the mandate of Uranus is revolution and stepping off the edge you can imagine that in our twenties we are challenged to break away from the ideals and even the communities that held us as children. In a world where Diaspora is commonplace and travel has been so very accessible the effects of Uranus in our early twenties was often to throw a person into a new culture or political awareness. Some kind of revolution is to be expected.

When Uranus shows up it is time to thrust forward into the future without a clue as to what waits. Thinking back to the discovery of this planet it is interesting to conjecture that before Uranus was discovered the future wasn't as open-ended as it has been ever since. The eighteenth century brought the challenge of a world in so much flux that it became more commonplace for a child to become an adult in a different world than that of her parents. We have come to accept this as 'normal' in our modern way of life. But it wasn't always so. The notion of rebellion as a natural part of development for all human beings is a relatively new concept.

What Uranus says to each and every elder in its highly unique and individualistic way is basically the same for all. You cannot hold up the world anymore. (Could you ever? Was it just an illusion anyway?) The time has come to jump in. You are unique and you are one of many. Embrace the chaos!

This poem by Rumi [3] reminds me of how it feels when Uranus comes to call:

"Chickpea to Cook"
A chickpea leaps almost over the rim of the pot
where it's being boiled.
"Why are you doing this to me?"
The cook knocks him down with the ladle.
"Don't you try to jump out.
You think I'm torturing you.
I'm giving you flavor,
so you can mix with spices and rice
and be the lovely vitality of a human being.
Remember when you drank rain in the garden.
That was for this."
Grace first. Sexual pleasure,
then a boiling new life begins,
and the Friend has something good to eat.
Eventually the chickpea
will say to the cook,
"Boil me some more.
Hit me with the skimming spoon.
I can't do this by myself.
I'm like an elephant that dreams of gardens
back in Hindustan and doesn't pay attention
to his driver. You're my cook, my driver,
my way into existence. I love your cooking."

The cook says,
"I was once like you,
fresh from the ground. Then I boiled in time,
and boiled in the body, two fierce boilings.
My animal soul grew powerful.
I controlled it with practices,
and boiled some more, and boiled
once beyond that,
and became your teacher."

At sixty it is useful to cultivate the awareness of the willing chickpea in the pot. We have been boiled and we are still being cooked. We can't prevent it. We aren't in our twenties any more when the boiling began. We aren't about to ride off into the sunset or live happily ever after. We know too much. Even if we do travel more and enjoy the fruits of our labor in these times of cultural, ecological and global chaos everyone is becoming aware in ways they may not have been before that this kind of travel and endless expansion can't go on as if nothing is changing. These notions are intensified in a particular way as they dovetail with our own personal experience of aging. An inward shift is required no matter how we act outwardly.

Uranus is specifically associated with the cutting edge of technology. In the first years of the twenty-first century this edge is shifting from moment to moment. It seems that by the time we master each new level of technology it has become almost obsolete and something new is required. Perhaps we can find some clues of what kind of consciousness is required to navigate this chaos in the realm of quantum physics. Here are some symbolic and poetic musings on the quantum reality of our moment of transition from adult to elder:

Uranus encourages us to realize that we are neither particle nor wave. As we get older perhaps we think we would like to feel more like a particle—physically measurable and safe within our limits. But the very opposite is true. Each and every day we experience the trough and the crest of a new and essentially unpredictable wave of change. We feel this through our losses and physical changes as well as via revelations about what life is *really* about. We truly have moments of realizing how youth is wasted on the young because they are so unaware. Now we are aware and like a wave we seem to have an almost infinite amount of possible manifestations. However our possibilities are limited because we are also the particle. We exist in this body and we need to respect that too. At sixty we have a lot in common with those in their early twenties and, then again, we don't. There is no working it out. You just have to jump into the madness of it all and be cooked.

Some of us meet the challenge of Uranus with a sense of defiance. We want to take on Nature Herself. Here is an interesting rebellion. How does one rebel against the physical limits of matter? We may play more tennis or take more supplements, go back to school or spend a lot more time at the gym. Within reason this makes sense yet Uranus seems to offer a more cosmic kind of revolution. In this life you are never too old to make a difference. What will you do with this potential in your elder years? How will you rock the status quo? There is of course no prescription for this. Some people do it simply by the way that they live and think and how that affects the people around them. Others take on society in a more general way through some kind of activism. It is easy as an elder to feel invisible in Western society. In fact you are not invisible at all. Your very presence in a situation reminds people that one day they too will grow older. It falls to the current crop of elders to stimulate the awareness that there is something of value in this stage of life. Uranus suggests it is time to break out of old, worn-out modes of thinking and see the world through the eyes of this new reality that endlessly presents to us. At fifty you were an old adult engaged in completing the task of being an adult. At sixty you are a new elder in a world engaged in chaotic change from which there is no return. We cannot get to know it so much as we can learn to live with the ever shifting sands of what we call reality.

It is an interesting phenomenon that many baby boomers and people younger may not have the option or the desire to go quietly into retirement. For many reasons from the disturbing reality of economic crises to the wonderful promise of a longer life span and greater vitality than the elders of yesteryear, it seems that the trend is away from retirement and toward "re-tire-ment": getting new tires. It is not as uncommon as it once was to see people in their 60s starting new careers or at least using creative means to hold on to what they have got.

A major part of crossing any threshold is about letting go of that which is familiar. This letting go can bring on a kind of madness. We have moments when we feel mad and possibly even free. Mad is an interesting word. It can mean angry as well as crazy. And when Uranus offers a challenge we often get the sense that we must decide if we will be angry or crazy. When we were looking at Saturn we considered how Saturn as the last planet visible to the naked eye protects us from the "madness" of the outer planets (the ones which cannot be seen without aid of telescopes). When Uranus comes it's clear that in some way we have left the known world which Saturn represents. Hopefully we are grounded enough to revel in the wild possibility that Uranus brings.

Before you can change the world around you, you must deal with the revolution that is going on inside you. There is the body thing; the getting older. This hits some people harder than others. People develop strategies to cope with these changes. They drink less alcohol, eat less junk food, take medication and exercise. All of these things help but there is a sense that one never quite finds permanent equilibrium on a physical level. We need rather to be aware of the shifting sands of day-to-day reactions to how our bodies feel.

Even more Uranian perhaps can be the little and big frustrations of the moment. We live in an age when the technology that you are so proud of understanding in year one has become obsolete by year three. One of the most universally despised aspects of the Uranus square is our increasing dependence on technical support. And then there are the minor but persistent frustrations such as the machine that doesn't work, the driving you don't want to do, the kids that don't live up to your expectations and/or the husband who snores. All these things test the limits of our ability to live peacefully in the moment. We have been in the habit of holding tight and making these things work. As we step into the Uranus challenge we are asked each and every time we meet a glitch, a frustration point, to leap into the unknown; to wake up to the realization that we are not the same person as the one who has been coping all these years. In a fundamental way we don't know exactly who we have become. Of course we can choose to ignore the flash of awareness but that is no doubt, costly in the end. (Appendix II: Exercises: Uranus Chapter 7)

Esther reflects back to the time of her early sixties as a time of social reorganization. Friends were leaving the city, and this necessitated a change to find some new ones, which brought Esther into activities that were new and challenged to some extent her existing ideology. In retrospect, the sense of being stretched to see the world from a different place was worth the discomfort.

Linda's Uranian challenge comes from the mental stress of her life much of which she ascribes to the computer. There is too much to sort through in a day and her mind must remain plugged in long after her body demands to unplug. The most frustrating thing about this for her is that it seems that every solution she comes up with entangles her even further in the technological morass. She may appreciate this threshold more after she is safely on the other side!

For Kate this challenge is far into the future. What she knows from her life thus far is that the thing she finds most disturbing is emotional chaos. She thrives when the family is stable. She can imagine, with some anxiety and a little curiosity, that this would be where she might meet the challenge. Without anticipating 'the worst' she realizes that a challenge here as she turns sixty would help her to let go of her need to control other people—for their own good of course—and that might be a good thing.

Until we are sixty I think the inclination may be to hold on even if it feels as though your knuckles are turning white. At sixty it seems more obvious that some letting go will offer greater freedom. As Uranus comes the sense is that you have no choice but to let go in any case. Even if you want to hold on, you can't. It's wonderful. It's horrible. If we perceive life, especially it's glitches and inconsistencies, as a kind of spiritual practice we may be fortunate every once in a while to experience the revelation that we are neither particle nor wave so to speak, we are always in the process of becoming. Each time we navigate our fear of that which we cannot control or predict, each time we let go into the unknown we let go of fear.

The influence of Uranus is not that of a hero who leaps into the fray such as Mighty Mouse and saves the day. This is not the way it offers to help us let go of fear. Uranus vanquishes fear through revelation and understanding that *this is it.* This wild, unpredictable, chaotic dance is Life. It always has been and it always will be. Each and every revelation that we experience shifts our perception of reality the way a turn of the wrist shifts the pattern in a kaleidoscope; we cannot stem the tide. Sometimes we feel akin to the grass, mowed down by the thresher and other times we are as the dust mote floating on the air. If we have worldly power we may feel like the thresher rather than the threshed but at sixty whether we admit it or not we know it is just a matter of time before we too will be eaten by life's unpredictable, awesome, awe-full power. How much better it is to take up the offer of glimpsing this than to deny such a powerful revelation. To never consciously participate in this dance is to miss out on one of life's most terrible and wonderful gifts.

Fear not, says Uranus. Not because you are safe but because life is (and has always been) a near death experience. If we take the challenge we inevitably become more conscious; more awakened. The aspect which Uranus makes to itself at the age of sixty constellates our need to *deal* with change. To quote Marian Woodman on the subject:

> If we can hold that tension, it can release the dancing star. That edge of chaos is where we think, "All that I believe in, all that I have trusted, all that I have known to be my truth is being taken away from me; I can no longer control my life; other forces are taking over." If at that point we can hold and recognize those forces that are coming in, then we can become a dancing star.[4]

If, as I believe, there is one thing elders are meant to do it is to rock the status quo. And the most powerful way to do that is to let go of fear. Letting go of fear when you are in your sixties and beyond however is very different than the fearlessness of people who are ignorant of experience. At this stage we are letting go of fear after a lifetime of experiencing danger. We let go of fear with full knowledge of what it means to suffer. As Granny Weatherwax says: "Fools rush in, but they are laggards compared to little old ladies with nothing left to fear." [5]

Consider the popular greeting card wisdom ascribed to author Catherine Aird: "If you can't be a good example, you will just have to be a horrible warning." Even if we make the terrible choice to shrivel up in a bitter, old corner when we are elders and wag, whine and point we are still an inspiration or at least a warning to people around us. Uranus asks us to consider how we might choose to rock the status quo of our world, our families, our communities, our countries and beyond even as our very own personal version of the status quo is being rocked within and without us. A wonderful example of this is the Grandmothers to Grandmothers Campaign of the Stephen Lewis Foundation [6]. This organization has created a link between Canadian and African Grandmothers. It seeks to create awareness and support for the African Grandmothers who are raising the 11 million Aids orphans of Africa.

Our specific experience of Uranus in the surrounding culture is something we might refer to as *the schism.* This is the double message we get from the world around us at least here in the developed world. On one hand we are the privileged. Based on the wonders of modern science we can look forward to living to 100. We have medicine and if that doesn't work we have a myriad of alternatives. We believe we are heading to the cure for cancer and more. We can watch our diet and exercise, and if that doesn't work we can take a pill. One of the most amazing areas of study available to us as we become elders in these times of great change are the constant advances in quantum physics and consciousness study. Consider the works of Barbara Marx Hubbard and the Foundation for Conscious Evolution. [7] If people can understand the universe as brilliantly as they do we must be evolving in a sustainable way.

On the other side of our schism we have global warming, global dimming, terrorism, war, peak oil, and the threat of pandemics that will decimate us sooner or later. Pesticides and air pollution, earthquakes, hurricanes and maybe worst of all, corruption that goes so deep it's to be expected. We also have social institutions that are crumbling even as you sit here and read this. The children seem lost and what kind of adults will they become with their heads full of violent imagery which they get off computers and video games not to mention their bodies full of drugs? It's a bleak future from this perspective.

On any given day you can turn on the radio or TV or read the paper and you will be bombarded with both sides of this as if it is kind of normal rather than something that could make you feel mad. We hear it all. We are conditioned to take it in and go about business as usual but it affects us. It's not the same thing as paradox. It's more like colliding realities. When you are under the influence of Uranus astrologically it can be tempting to try and live in denial about this schism but truly this adds even more tension to an already tense, irreconcilable amount of input bombarding our minds.

We just can't make all this information add up; nor should we. Most likely it wasn't this way for our ancestors. Did they feel overwhelmed? My guess is that by and large they accepted themselves as part of nature more easily than we do (at least before Uranus was discovered in the eighteenth century). Their ability to filter out what didn't add up would have been stronger because they were not plugged in. The feeling of living in a schism has gotten progressively worse over the last 300 years.

As the basic unit of society the family becomes less and less of a container for the young and the old who need it the most, we are thrown headlong into the 'new'. Hopefully as quantum physics suggest this chaos is ultimately taking us to a higher level of order. Possibly we will emerge on the other side of chaos to a place where our planet and its inhabitants can live more sanely than we have done in the past. (Appendix: Exercises: Uranus)

When we speak of the power of Uranus in our eldering journey it suggests that we are challenged to live in a tumultuous present; an ever more intensely changing *now.* To accomplish this presence we must also foster an attitude of forgiveness. At one level, forgiveness seems specific. We must forgive our parents for their mistakes. We must forgive our ex-partners, our friends and associates who have betrayed us. We must forgive ourselves for our bad choices and our ignorance. In the end, though, all these specific acts of forgiveness make it clear that it is Life Itself that we must forgive. Somehow it brought us here and even if it lived up to all our expectations, which is unlikely, it still will end. Now there is a betrayal to be reckoned with.

Being an elder takes courage and one of the most courageous acts of all is to forgive this imperfect world that we may be free from the bondage of blame be it subtle or overt. For as Helen Luke so eloquently has said:

> In other words, it is the breakthrough of forgiveness, in its most profound sense—universal and particular, impersonal and personal—that alone brings the "letting go" the ultimate freedom of the spirit. For in the moment of that realization, every false guilt whether seen as one's own or as other people's, is gone forever. The real guilt, which each of us carries—the refusal to see, to be aware—is accepted. So we may look open-eyed at ourselves and the world and suffer the pain and joy of the divine conflict, which is the human condition, the meaning of incarnation. Every so-called blow of fate becomes, as it were, an essential note in the music of God, however discordant it may sound to our superficial hearing. [8]

In her book *Crones Don't Whine,* Jean Shinoda Bolen sums it up this way:

> A lifetime is the material that each of us has to work with. Until this span is over, we are still in process, in the midst of an unfinished story. What we do with our lives is our magnum opus, or great work of personal creativity. If we acquire a crone's-eye view, then we will see ourselves and others from the perspective of soul rather than ego. Aging well is a goal worth wanting." And "The crone is a potential, much like an inherent talent, that needs to be recognized and practiced in order to develop. This wise presence in your psyche will grow, once you trust that there is a crone within and begin to listen. [9]

Here is an overview of what I think astrology suggests as signposts for becoming and being elders.

Elderhood is a period when the (capital) Self attempts to distill itself from the (small) self. This distillation process has something and everything to do with the slowing down of the body. This is not about a body that doesn't work; it is about paying more attention to the body we have inhabited all these years and not taking it for granted. If we cannot become truly mindful of ourselves and therefore fully present in our physical body, our consciousness shrivels. If we honor the still, small voice within as is required, our consciousness has the opportunity to expand. If the greatest love affair on the planet is between the body and the soul, at 60 and beyond is the time to overthrow the status quo that keeps you from realizing this and to really inhabit your physical body even as you become aware that one day they must part. It is nothing less than a revolution in consciousness that is asked of us.

(For an exercise pertaining to Uranus, see Appendix II: Chapter 7: Uranus.)

Chapter 8

The Path Less Traveled

To describe the vast unexplored regions on their maps, the ancient cartographers wrote, "Here there be dragons." This chapter is about exploring the unexplored, entering into the unknown. Welcome to Dragon Territory.

In our ever-changing, chaotic world-in-flux it often seems as though there is no end to information. But there comes a moment in the study of all subjects when you have enough information and the time arrives when you must sit in silence to see what you have learned. This is that time.

Before you make yourself cozy, before you curl up to read the story I am going to tell, take one last journey through the material we have covered. You aren't looking for anything in particular. You are certainly not looking for answers or "the Answer." It is more like you are looking to see if you even know the question; you are cultivating an overview, a broad perspective on life.

Over the time it took you to get to this last chapter you have considered many archetypal concepts. First there was the whole notion that an adult is not the same as an elder. Then we considered what kind of foundation we might create to hold us as emerging elders. After that was an exploration of the personality and how it holds you back or enables you to get where you want to go. Then we considered our heart's desire and our basic assumptions. From there we journeyed through the territory of body and soul, the tricky realm of responsibility and what is and is not required of us. After that we explored the notion of madness and the chaos itself. And now we are here.

When I teach this material in person, I gather the participants together on the last evening and conduct a ritual for them to help integrate the information.[1] Rather than describe a ritual, I have decided to tell you a story that includes the aspects of the ritual and allows you to make the journey along with the main character.

Once upon a time not so long ago and not too far from here, a woman decided that the time had come for her to go on a journey. This woman looked a lot like you. She was your age and height and she had the same kind of hair. She wore the same shoes as you wear when you go for a long walk. This woman wears a cape made of indigo, embroidered with stars and planetary glyphs. This cape affords excellent protection from the elements when needed and can be used as bedding at night. It has pockets that hold food and drink as well as medicine and art supplies. In short, it's a magic cape.

We will call this woman Lily, and we know that she was named for the greatest Grandmother of them all: Lilith[2], the first woman.

She had always known that this moment would come, that one day she would outgrow her comfortable little house filled with all the things she loves and then it would be time. But knowing that this day would come isn't the same as actually setting out. The journey will inevitably be different from what she imagines.

Perhaps she will be tested the way Baba Yaga tested Vasalisa. It won't be the test of the hero. It will be a test she cannot pass or fail. Only she will listen, hear and eventually in some way be changed by her experience. Meaning may not come till much later, if at all. Most important, she thinks, will be to stay open, in the heart and to the senses. Let her who has ears to hear, hear.

In this way people down through the ages have made themselves available to the wisdom of Nature.

No, this will be no ordinary journey. She isn't going to see the attractions, to taste the local specialties or to put a notch in her belt for another sacred site revealed. This is not the journey of the tourist nor even the traveler. This is the way of the pilgrim. As such she knows that there is no end to this journey, for the end will be a threshold leading to the beginning of another journey. And so it will be till the very end.

As she waits for the sun to rise she prepares by smudging herself with sage. In the dark her match flares and she ignites the dry and fragrant herb in the shell she holds in her other hand. Smoke rises from the shell and fills the air with the earthy smell that connects her to the eons of women who have burned smudge before her. She moves the smoking shell up and down her body as if washing herself with smoke. When she is done, she sits and waits in the darkness.

Sitting isn't as easy as it looks. She is restless and her nose itches. Her mind begins to spin and although she doesn't move, many thoughts rise up like flocks of unruly birds. She is filled with dread at the enormity of what lies before her as well as the impossibility of turning away from it. Just as she is about to turn and run from this place, she remembers a moment long ago when she was little, when everything was safe and warm and she wondered what it was like outside the circle of her comfort. She remembers her mother and her grandmother. She remembers her mother speaking of her grandmother. She knows herself as the daughter of all these mothers. Her breathing calms. Her mind stills. She is ready.

As Lily relaxes she opens her eyes and notices that the sky is just beginning to lighten. The first rays have arrived and she stands up and walks toward the east. As she walks she calls on the powers of the east. She opens herself to the possibility of new beginnings and the power of inspiration.

As day arrives Lily is thrilled by the way the trees begin to come to life. The ground beneath her feet, which had been in shadows, is suddenly alive with details. The sky before her is moving from black to gray and rays of brilliant color begin to bring the world back to life. Birdsong surrounds her and she is filled with joy. Suddenly, without knowing how she got here, Lily realizes she has come to a fork in the road. It's like the letter Y—behind her is the stem of the letter. To her left one choice and to her right another. Squatting low to the ground, in a dark dress and so still as to be almost unnoticed, is an old woman. The word hag crosses Lily's mind. There she sits; the old woman with her broom and her pile of bones, her snaggletooth grin and her wispy white hair, her eyes as sharp as an eagle's, filled with insight and deadly aim for what prey, Lily cannot or will not imagine. Lily has a vivid memory of the tales of Baba Yaga that her mother used to tell. The old woman stands and is taller than Lily expected—taller, straighter and stronger. She speaks to our heroine, "Why should *you* cross? Do you even know the difference between the world in which you have lived and the world beneath? Can you even tell if you are alive or dead? Awake or asleep?" She is frightening and challenging and yet so familiar.

Standing at the fork in the road Lily looks to the left and to the right. These are the choices and she has no idea which way is the way. She falls to her knees and says what she never before knew to say, "I call on the power of the triple goddess, she who stands at the crossroads—all crossroads. You who have been here to guide me into and out of the underworld. You who existed before the world in which I live and will continue to exist as long as there is a world. I implore you to infuse me with your presence. Give me a glimpse of your true nature. Help me to see with your eyes, to understand with your knowledge, to feel with your depth."

Lily is suddenly filled with the awareness that this is all she has ever wanted, to have this old woman grant her permission to pass.

As Lily finishes speaking she opens her eyes. The old woman has vanished and the sun has risen much higher in the sky. Without a trace of doubt Lily turns toward the south. The sun is in fact approaching noon. She is so happy to have passed through the gate that she skips on toward the south aware of the birds and the animals who live in the forest, aware now that she is in a forest. She was so absorbed in her purpose, so focused on the possibility that she might not make it across the threshold (although she didn't know this) that she wasn't truly aware of her surroundings. Now she is filled with joy at the warm sun and the tall trees dressed in their green leaves. She rejoices in the smells of summer fruits and the swirling dance of animals, plants and all the elements that surround her.

Ahead she sees a lake, blue and glassy in the noonday light. It seems like the perfect place for lunch. Lily finds a rock on which to sit and in one of the many pockets of her cape finds some bread and cheese, an apple and a bottle of water—each one a delight because she is hungry and thirsty, and here is food and drink.

As Lily sits on her rock, eating her lunch, her mind drifts toward a question she has sometimes pondered: Is there one goddess or many? There is only one mother . . . one egg . . . Drowsy and satisfied, Lily makes herself comfortable inside her magic cape and falls asleep, into a dream of childhood. She sees her child hands, plump and buttery, reaching for the ball, the book, the moon. Suddenly the scene changes to a night on the beach when she is older. Warm daytime breezes have turned to chill; semi-naked bodies pull on sweatshirts and warm pants. Eyes meet, hands touch and suddenly she is awash in a sea of feelings. Her bare feet wiggle in the sand. She relaxes in drowsy, sweet languor by the fire after a day of swimming. Then the dream changes once more. She is a big sow giving birth to a litter of piglets. She rolls this way and that and her large pink body opens to release new life into the world. One little piglet looks up at her and laughs and suddenly, the face of her firstborn appears. She is a mother opening her arms to a sweet-smelling little one—to the Wheel of Life. She sees the Wheel of Fortune from the tarot emblazoned on the front of the baby's jumper. In her dream she becomes a bird and flies high over the sea looking for food. She swoops down, and there is her hand with its brown spots and protruding veins, more bony than wrinkled. She thinks she is the bird picking up the hand in her beak but in fact she is lifting it to shield her waking eyes from the sun that has moved to shine its mid-day heat onto her face.

One goddess or many? She leans over the water to wash the sleep from her eyes and she sees a woman staring back at her from the water. For a moment she believes it to be a mermaid; a great, mysterious creature that she had always believed existed but had never actually seen. In this face, her own face, for a fleeting moment she sees the face of the one who began this life, the one who carries it and the one who will take it to the end. There is one goddess who is many. And looking into the face of her life and her death she understands that she is one and the same as that goddess. For an infinite moment she is filled and whole. She knows a joy too large for her body to hold; a fire that burns, even as it delights. And the moment passes, and she is just Lily. Just Lily. Not more, not less.

There is only one mystery and we all share in it. The details of our stories may be different, but we all are the same. We are born, we grow old and we die. This is the mystery. In the south on a sunny day, after a good lunch by a beautiful lake, this seems a glorious truth.

Lily stands and shakes out pieces of grass and twigs that attached themselves to her cape while she rested by the lake. She notices that the sun has moved from the mid-heaven down to the west. The shadows aren't long yet but they will be. She pulls her cape around her after putting her things back in its big pockets and she turns her feet toward the west. She is delighted with the realization that though there is only one mystery there are innumerable ways to know it. Each of us is like a facet on a diamond, reflecting the light in our own unique way. This is why we tell stories, make art, fall in love with the wrong people as well as the right ones. No matter who we are, the dance of our lives expresses this light. It is truly a wonderful thing.

The path, once so clear and wide seems suddenly to have become thinner, less traveled. As Lily walks on she sees to the left in the dark of the woods, a wild cat tearing into the flesh of its prey. A little while later, she sees a hawk rising up from the ground with a mouse in its beak. She pulls her cloak around her shoulders and hurries on. As the shadows lengthen she realizes she has been walking for hours. The air is cooler, the terrain more marshy and there are not many good places to sit. She is glad for her cloak and reassured by the fact that it has a hood she will use later on. Mostly she walks with her head down, making sure that she doesn't stumble on the path but as she looks up she notices in some of the trees a spot of red, some yellow here and there. The leaves are changing color. It is as though a great painter with a delicate and deliberate brush is turning the green to red, yellow and orange. She is moved by this and saddened that she is alone and there is no one with whom she can share this subtle beauty. What was she thinking when she set out on this journey alone? Why did she leave her comfy home and her good friends, the ones who love her and know her? What will all this journeying achieve?

She has no answer. She remembers the old woman she met at the crossroads and the joy of seeing her own reflection in the lake. They seem like peak moments, each one a beautiful bead in her hand which she cannot seem to string into a necklace. Her longing fills her to the brim and pulls her on toward the west. It is a burden she carries and the weight of it leads her mind toward regret for the failures of her life which seem plentiful. Suddenly she is aware of all the ways she could have done better by her parents, her children, her partner, her intellectual achievements, her spirituality. She could have listened more, been kinder, worked harder. Nothing has been as stellar as she thought it could or would be. The way is filled with regret and sorrow.

Feeling as though her life has been pointless, she comes to a field bordered by a stand of trees in the north. She finds a rock—at last, something to sit upon. Weary from the path that was never quite clear, unsure if she is where she should be, exhausted from her ruminations, she sits down and without thinking looks up into the biggest sky she has ever seen. Giant, sweeping clouds of whipped cream white, swathed in wispy strands of gray fill only a portion of the sky around the south and west horizons. The big yellow sun hovers over the west, readying for its journey down under. As Lily looks around she sees the last white and purple cosmos flowers of the season standing bravely if a bit ragged; leaning toward the south. She sees hollyhock seed pods that once were flowers, brown and dead-looking on their stalks; ready to fall to the earth and wait through a long dark winter before they spring back to life again. It makes her weary, even as she is filled with a sense of deep longing and awed by the beauty of her surroundings. For a moment it seems to her that the world is perfectly still. Then her ears awaken and she hears a massive song that fills the air—insects and birds going vigorously about their end-of-day business. How is it that she was never before able to hear such a symphony? Even her sense of smell comes alive, and she believes she senses the scent of transformation on the wind.

As Lily looks toward the sun, sinking closer to the horizon, she is filled with melancholy, an aching sadness so vast she can only bow her head as the tears fall to the ground. If someone asked her she would not be able to tell them why she is crying except to say, "It all seems so sad." And if they asked her what "it" is that seems so sad, she could only imagine the answer would be life. Not my life but all life; so sad and so beautiful. It makes no sense. With all her heart she wants the sun to stay even as the sky becomes a work of art created by something so vast and infinite it cannot be known. Her longing moves her to look for something she can offer to the setting sun. She should leave a stone or a piece of her life; some jewelry or a poem to honor this awful beauty. Her pockets are empty except for crusts of bread and some water. She worries if she will have enough to eat for the rest of the journey. In the end, all she can offer the setting sun seems to be her tears.

What Lily doesn't know is that after she turns away from the sunset and picks herself up to continue her journey to the north something happened. Where each tear fell a big red poppy sprang up, delicate and wild, flower of eternal sleep.

Walking north as early evening turns to night, Lily is lost inside her mind. She follows the path with confidence despite the fact that it is a moonless night and the path has become even narrower than it was. She is stunned by the power of her feelings and their contradictory nature. She feels despair at the thought that beauty and sorrow are so connected. How is it she never knew this? Or did she know it but not *know* it? Suddenly her reverie is broken as she trips over a root and falls flat on her face, in the dark, on the cold, moist ground. Luckily her cape breaks the fall and she is not hurt but she is put on notice. The way is dark and she must pay attention. As Lily stands up she sees that the trees in this part of the forest are closer and bigger than those in the woods she passed through before. This is truly the forest primeval. She remembers the wild cat ripping into its prey and she shudders hoping the magic in the cape will protect her from predators. Her footsteps become a meditation and she loses track of time and distance. All of existence is bound up in walking, walking through the night.

Gradually, without consciously realizing it at first, Lily becomes aware of a sound like drumming. It's a simple rhythmic beat, like a heartbeat. One and two three, one and two three, steady and growing louder as she walks on. Having emptied herself of sorrow at the sunset she realizes she must have let go of fear as well because she is drawn to the drumming and not anxious about whom the drummers might be. She thinks it must be the very heartbeat of the forest to which she is drawn.

The narrow path suddenly turns a sharp right, and there in a grove of trees are eight women. Each wears a cape not unlike Lily's. Their hoods are up and Lily wonders how she knows they are women. But she knows that she knows. She steps easily to the outside edge of the circle and the women lift their heads and shrug off their hoods. Lily is shocked to see her mother and her grandmother. She recognizes her great-grandmother from a photo she has seen. As she gazes at the faces of the rest of the women she sees that each of them resembles the others. One woman looks so old and frail with her wispy white hair and her birdlike face that Lily wonders if these women are alive at all. Before she can work this out in her mind the eldest woman comes forward and says, "Welcome daughter." She reaches out her hands toward Lily and without thinking Lily reaches back and steps into the empty space in the circle that was waiting for her.

Although Lily is filled with questions, she knows better than to speak. The drum has not missed a beat. The oldest of the grandmothers looks around the circle at each woman. As her eyes come to rest on Lily she starts to speak.

"Once upon a time, so long ago that memory cannot find it. Before history, when the world was very young, it was ruled by four women. We might call them goddesses; we might just know them as women. Back then to rule the world was nothing like what you think of today. Back then to rule the world meant to hold the four corners of reality stable, to hold these corners stable so that life could flourish. The four goddesses who had this task each enjoyed the responsibilities, the duties and the pleasures of holding her corner. They enjoyed the fact that as each did what she was called to and as she met the efforts of the other three, life blossomed and bloomed everywhere.'

Lily is aware in some corner of her mind that the old woman is speaking in a voice that is deeply resonant with not a trace of age or frailty sounding in her words. She continues: "Times changed as times will and there came a time when the four goddesses were no longer welcomed in their duties. As humans came to the fore they created a way of ruling the world like nothing ever seen before. Three of the goddesses were allowed to remain, although their powers were greatly diminished and they were no longer permitted to hold the corners of the world. The fourth goddess, considered to be the greatest threat, was exiled and no one spoke her name for the longest time. For the sake of this story I will call this woman Persephone but she has many names. You may even know her as Lilith. Traces of her can be found in many tales."

Lily is surprised to hear her name spoken in the story. She is pulled even more deeply into the hypnotic tale of goddesses and ancient mysteries.

The old woman continues: "We think of Persephone as the maiden. We have been taught to think of her as the maiden who was abducted into the underworld. But the truth is once she entered the underworld, she was maiden no longer. The truth is that she was not abducted; she was drawn to the mystery of what lies below. The truth is that in the patriarchal world, this power of the feminine to descend by choice, to seek out the mysteries, is the single most inadmissible thing. And so the original story was changed."

Anger came through in these words, and Lily shuddered as she was reminded of the stories she had heard of her namesake.

The old woman went on: "The story of the willing descent of the maiden into the underworld was changed to a rape, and so her power was lost. It is up to the grandmothers to retrieve that power. It is up to the crones because when Persephone arrived in the underworld, eager to learn its secrets, her teacher was Hecate.[3] At the bottom of the descent there she stood, the old woman herself, stirring her cauldron—surrounded by the symbols and tools of her powerful magic, the magic of transformation. The same magic she uses to lead us in and out of the underworld, the magic that takes our lives and turns them into something of which we are not aware.

"So who is Persephone in these times? She is the marginalized woman, the woman at the edge. She is the one you seek when you are troubled, but whom you deny by the light of day. She is the part of each and every one of you that knows and sees and feels the other world.

"Persephone confuses you in these times in which you live. You fall into the overwhelming belief that if you see, if you know, you must do something about what you see. *But the power of this kind of seeing is in the seeing itself.*

"In the underworld doing only gets in the way of seeing, being present and knowing. In the underworld the quality of thinking is a liability not an asset. In the underworld the books are made of rock and stone, of moisture and wind; of light and shadow. In the underworld the greatest secret is the most obvious thing, yet no one sees it.

"You are not here to be stewards of nature; you are not here to appreciate nature. You are Nature itself. As elders and ancestors you have experienced the nooks and crannies of your marginalized selves for thousands of years. You have felt at a loss for your children and the ones you love and the ones you don't even know, who are denied and neglected, abandoned and scorned. You have seen the dark shadow of ecological disaster and you sense the coming crises.

"As elders you also see and sense the possibilities. You know within your own lives and the lives of these same people who touch you, the incredible power and wisdom of nature to regenerate, to heal, to live on."

At this point the old woman looks around the circle. Her gaze falls on each of the other women in turn. Even so her eyes come back to Lily's. "You have invoked the power of the crossroads. Standing at the crossroads means you can see in all directions at once. The power of this seeing is a power in and of itself. If you speak the truth of what you see, what you sense, what you know, you will be like the butterfly that flaps its wings in the southern hemisphere and starts the storm in the north."

Lily is moved by these words. She doesn't know if she has heard them inside her head or through her ears. She is suddenly not sure if she is an elder or an ancestor. But she knows the truth for once, even as she experiences it. She is fully present to this moment. Her knowing is one with her experience and oddly enough, there are no words. Not one.

The women begin to dance in a circle. Lily joins in and as she does she realizes they are dancing her into the center of the circle. Each in turns comes to Lily and gives her something; one anoints her third eye, another blows smoke around her body, a third offers her water in a stone goblet. One stands before Lily and as their eyes meet Lily sees fires burning and feels seen to the core of her being. Another comes to Lily and places a stone in her hand. A stone so smooth and black, etched with a silvery crescent Moon. Before Lily can respond to any of these gifts, another woman comes to her with a big red poppy. As the last woman approaches Lily is aware that this is her actual grandmother. As she looks into her face she is amazed at how much they look alike. Her grandmother says, "Where there is no fear, there is no death. Welcome daughter."

Alone in the forest Lily wonders if she dreamed these grandmothers or if her experience was "real." She laughs at the absurdity of the distinction and looks down at her hands; one is clutching the black stone with the Moon etched in silver, the other is holding a bright red poppy.

Walking on toward the east, away from the grove of trees, Lily sees the very first hint of a new day beginning to dawn. She sits and waits.

And you, who have come to the end of the story and a journey of your own making, this is an excellent time to read the cards or choose a smooth stone or simply to sit and wait and see what comes.

(For an exercise to sum it all up, see Appendix II: Chapter 8.)

Appendix I

Horoscopes of the Elders: Key Words: Astrological Tables

Chapter 1

Esther: August 18, 1936 3:30 AM EDT New York, NY
Linda: May 12 1947 5:50 PM PDT Vancouver, BC
Kate: November 15, 1960 11:12 AM EST Toronto, ON

Esther Elder
Aug 18, 1936
New York,NY
03:30:00 AM EDT
ZONE: +04:00
074W00'23"
40N42'51"

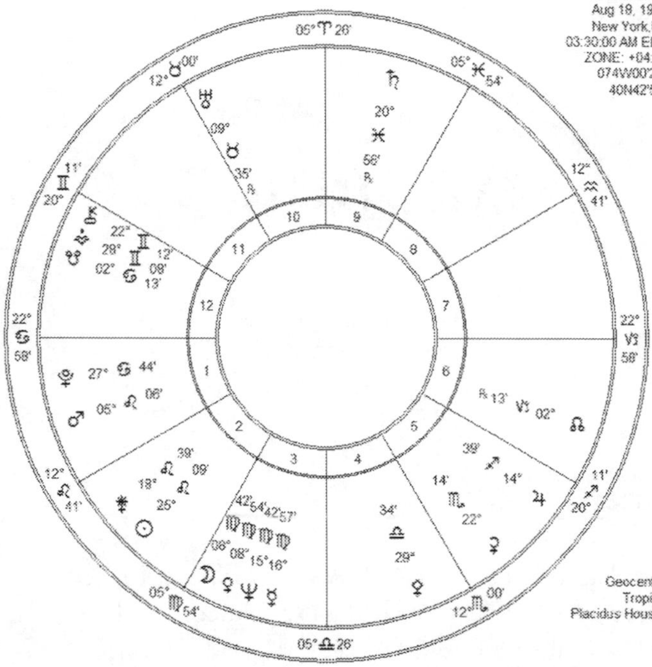

Geocentric
Tropical
Placidus Houses

Fir	Ear	Air	Wat
4	6	3	4

Crd	Fix	Mut
4	5	8

Zodiac Signs	Pl	Planet	Plan's Sign	Hous	Position
♈ Aries	☽	Moon	Virgo	3rd	08° ♍ 42'
♉ Taurus	☉	Sun	Leo	2nd	25° ♌ 09'
♊ Gemini	☿	Mercury	Virgo	3rd	16° ♍ 57'
♋ Cancer	♀	Venus	Virgo	3rd	08° ♍ 54'
♌ Leo	♂	Mars	Leo	1st	05° ♌ 06'
♍ Virgo	♃	Jupiter	Sagittarius	5th	14° ♐ 39'
♎ Libra	♄	Saturn	Pisces	9th	20° ♓ 56' ℞
♏ Scorpio	♅	Uranus	Taurus	10th	09° ♉ 35' ℞
♐ Sagittarius	♆	Neptune	Virgo	3rd	15° ♍ 42'
♑ Capricorn	♇	Pluto	Cancer	1st	27° ♋ 44'
♒ Aquarius	☊	Node	Capricorn	8th	02° ♑ 13' ℞
♓ Pisces	⚷	Chiron	Gemini	12th	22° ♊ 12'
	⚳	Ceres	Scorpio	5th	22° ♏ 14'

Julie Simmons
416 424 3079
julie@juliesimmons.ca
www.juliesimmons.ca
Toronto, Ontario

Linda Elder
May 12, 1947
Vancouver,CAN
05 50:00 PM PDT
ZONE: +07:00
123W07'00"
49N16'00"

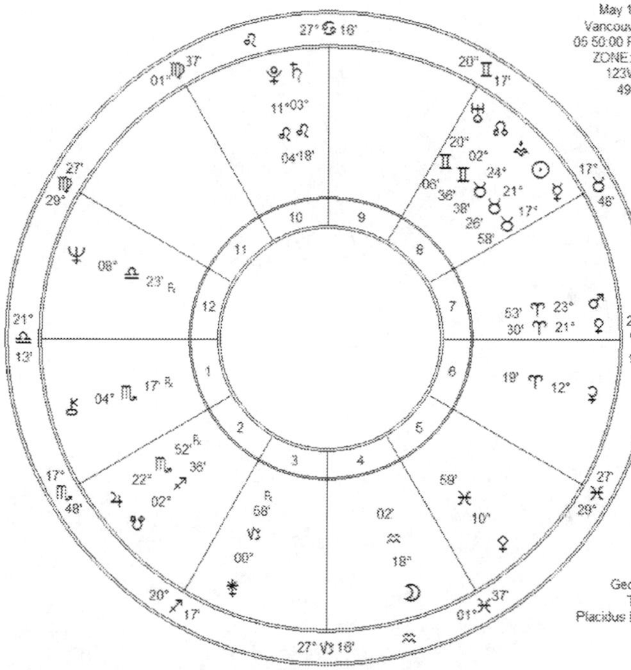

Geocentric
Tropical
Placidus Houses

Fir	Ear	Air	Wat
6	4	4	3

Crd	Fix	Mut
5	8	4

Zodiac Signs	Pl	Planet	Plan's Sign	Hous	Position
♈ Aries	☽	Moon	Aquarius	4th	18°♒02'
♉ Taurus	☉	Sun	Taurus	8th	21°♉26'
♊ Gemini	☿	Mercury	Taurus	8th	17°♉58'
♋ Cancer	♀	Venus	Aries	7th	21°♈30'
♌ Leo	♂	Mars	Aries	7th	23°♈53'
♍ Virgo	♃	Jupiter	Scorpio	2nd	22°♏52'℞
♎ Libra	♄	Saturn	Leo	10th	03°♌18'
♏ Scorpio	♅	Uranus	Gemini	8th	20°♊06'
♐ Sagittarius	♆	Neptune	Libra	12th	08°♎23'℞
♑ Capricorn	♇	Pluto	Leo	10th	11°♌04'
♒ Aquarius	☊	Node	Gemini	8th	02°♊36'
♓ Pisces	⚷	Chiron	Scorpio	1st	04°♏17'℞
	⚳	Ceres	Aries	8th	12°♈19'

Julie Simmons
416 424 3079
julie@juliesimmons.ca
www.juliesimmons.ca
Toronto, Ontario

Fir	Ear	Air	Wat
1	5	1	5

Crd	Fix	Mut
6	5	1

Kate Elder
Nov 15, 1960
Toronto,CAN
11:12:59 AM EST
ZONE: +05:00
079W23'00"
43N39'00"

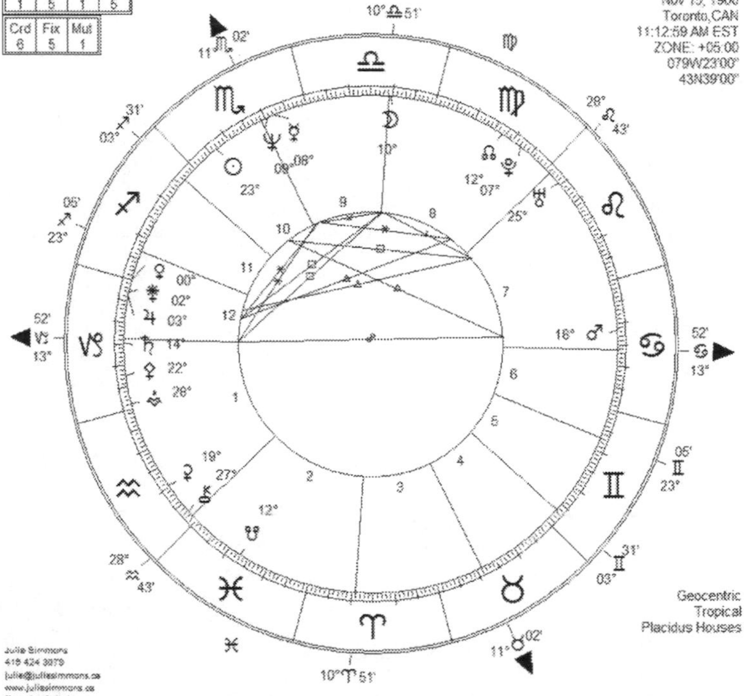

Geocentric
Tropical
Placidus Houses

Julie Simmons
416 424 3079
julie@juliesimmons.ca
www.juliesimmons.ca
Toronto Ontario

Pl	Position	Hous	Digni
☽	10° ♎24'	8th	
☉	23° ♏18'	10th	
☿	08° ♏08' ℞	9th	
♀	00° ♑22'	12th	
♂	18° ♋29'	7th	Fall
♃	03° ♑51'	12th	Fall
♄	14° ♑40'	1st	Ruler
♅	25° ♌42'	7th	Detri
♆	09° ♏24'	9th	
♇	07° ♍58'	8th	
☊	12° ♍57' ℞	8th	
⚷	27° ♒27'	1st	
⚳	19° ♒38'	1st	

Julian Day: 2437254.17568
Obliq. Eclip: +23° 26'31"
The 320th day of the year.
LMT: 10:55:27
UT: 16:12:59
UT-LMT: 05:17:32
ST: 14h34m26s
RAMC: 218° 36'
DeltaT: 33.10"
Planetary Hour: Moon (☽)
5th Hour of Mars-Day
Sunrise (aprox.): 07:17 EST
Sunset (aprox.): 16:47 EST
Adjusted Calculation Dates
0h= Mar 14 12h= Sep 12

House Cusps:	
01	13° ♑52'
02	28° ♒43'
03	10° ♈51'
04	11° ♉02'
05	03° ♊31'
06	23° ♊05'
07	13° ♋52'
08	28° ♌43'
09	10° ♎51'
10	11° ♏02'
11	03° ♐31'
12	23° ♐05'

Aspects:			
☊☍☋	0°00's	♄△☊	1°43's
☿⚹♇	0°10'a	♄⚹☋	1°43's
☽∠♅	0°18'a	♅☍⚷	1°45'a
♇⚼⚴	0°44'a	⚳∠⚵	1°49'a
♃∠⚳	0°47's	☉□♅	2°23'a
⚶∠☋	0°54's	♀☌⚵	2°27'a
☊⚼⚶	0°54's	⚴⚹⚷	2°55's
☽⚺♆	0°58's	♀☌♃	3°29'a
♃☌⚵	1°01'a	♆⚹☊	3°33'a
☉⚹⚴	1°04's	♆△☋	3°33'a
♂⚻⚳	1°09's	☉□⚳	3°40's
☿☌♆	1°16's	♂☍⚴	3°46's
⚷⚺⚶	1°24's	♂☍♄	3°48'a
♆⚹♇	1°26's	♃△♇	4°08'a
♀⚺⚶	1°31's	☉□⚷	4°08'a

KEY WORDS

Some key words I have developed over thirty years as an astrologer are listed below. I also recommend *Key Words for Astrology* by Hajo Banzhaf and Anna Haebler (Newburyport, MA: Weiser, 1996).

SIMPLE KEY WORDS FOR SIGNS

Aries: I am. Individuality.
Energetic, pioneering, dynamic, reckless, impatient, demanding.

Taurus: I have. Values. Pleasure.
Practical, sensual, invests time, energy, money and love what they truly value, lethargic, self-indulgent, dull.

Gemini: I think. Learning. Language. Communication.
Clever, curious, charming, quick, agile, superficial, amoral, fickle, distracted, phony.

Cancer: I need. Feeling (not the same as emotion). Bonding. Nesting.
Tenacious, ambition driven by feeling, caretaker, sensitive, devoted, fear of abandonment, need to be needed, escape into dream world or depression, wishful thinker, emotional blackmailer.

Leo: I will. Creativity. Self-expression. Self-esteem.
Calm, self-reliant, risk-taker, self-confident, generous, creative, entrepreneur, narcissistic, megalomaniac, condescending, self-important.

Virgo: I adjust. To analyze. Seeking meaning in every-day reality.

Efficient, diligent, practical but shrewd, reserved, critical, fussy, perfectionist, detail-obsessed, fault finding mania.

Libra: I relate. Negotiation. Debate. Justification. Harmony. Diplomatic, tolerant, stylish, influenced by form and harmony, debater, negotiator, unable to make decisions, competitive, indecisive, superficial, denial as a way of life.

Scorpio: I transform (whatever it takes), desire, initiation. Perceptive and uncompromising, breaker of taboos, profound and unyielding in the quest for truth, inscrutable, passionate, tyrannical, destructive, dogmatic, fixated, jealous, vindictive.

Sagittarius: I see. Vision. Judgment. Discrimination. Enthusiastic, motivated, confident, visionary, constantly learning, free spirit, discriminating, show-off, vain, fanatic, dogmatic, fears criticism or disgrace, arrogant.

Capricorn: I use. Management. The right use of resources. Responsible for the good of all, diligent, persevering, dependable, practical, careful emotionally, mistrustful with feelings, drudge, rigid conservatism, reserved, melancholic, old before their time.

Aquarius: I know. Idealism. Idea-ism. Humanitarian. Friendly. Independent, considerate, perspective, idealistic, ingenious, rational, friendly, feel inferior, eccentric, armchair philosopher, exceedingly mental, misunderstood genius, anarchist, fear deep feelings, impersonal.

Pisces: I believe (in spite of no proof). Yearning. Oneness. Unfinished business.
Sensitive to others, empathetic, willing to sacrifice, great creative fantasy, psychic, fearful, victim, vague, cruel, addictive, easily seduced, depressive, masochistic.

Julie Simmons—March 2000 with help from ***Keywords for Astrology:*** Banzhaf & Haebler

SIMPLE KEY WORDS FOR PLANETS AND POINTS

Sun: Father (parent who takes you out into the world), what you take pride in, your heart's desire.
Moon: Mother, how you get your needs met, emotional response.
Moon phase: The relationship between the Sun and the Moon when you were born. Think of it as the container within which the chart sits, an indication of personality type, your general style of relationship.
Ascendant: How you survive, your defensive posture, personality, the way you look.
Venus: Love and beauty, values, women.
Jupiter: Abundance, luck, judgment, deep held fundamental beliefs about yourself and life in general, religious leaders, teachers, gurus.
Saturn: Authority, responsibility, restriction, restraint, discipline, the boss—what you can, can't and must do.
Uranus: Prometheus (where you steal from the gods to change your life, just because you can), revelation, revolution, political groups, friends, social groups, breakthrough.
North Node: The thing you reach for but aren't quite comfortable with.
South Node: The habits of many lifetimes.

MORE EXTENSIVE KEYWORDS:

Planets

☉ The Sun:

Principles: Will, Life, Vitality, Purpose, Day, Consciousness, Father(ing), Power, Aspiration, The Future.

Drives: To role-play, to be, to express oneself, to create, to individuate, to stand out, to lead to command

Needs: Validation, acknowledgment, acceptance, recognition, self-expression, risk, prominence, status.

Existential questions: Who Am I: What is my purpose and my heart's desire? Can I be myself? What am I becoming? How am I special?

☽ The Moon:

Principles: Emotion, Needs, instincts, mother(ing), the family, home, security/insecurity, habits, subconscious, (night consciousness), the past.

Drives: To be receptive, to belong, to bond, to feel, to react, to support and be supported, to root to merge, to nest.

Needs: Basic—food, shelter, safety, comfort, connection, belonging.

Existential questions: What do I need? Where is My Home? Who (what) is my family? Where am I rooted? Can my needs be met in the world? Who can I get to mother me?

☿ Mercury

Principles: Intelligence, communication, mind, language, logic, reasoning, learning, dexterity, mobility, curiosity, exchange of information and ideas.

Drives: To communicate, to learn, to name, to classify and categorize, to analyze, to perceive.

Needs: stimulation, interest, variety, information, someone to listen and talk to.

Existential Questions: What's happening around me? What do I think? How is it all connected? What do I want to learn?

♀ Venus

Principles: Love, harmony, balance, interaction, relating, sensuality, value (worth), art, aesthetics, social decorum & tact.

Drives: To relate, to attract, to be valued, to beautify, or refine.

Needs: Physical and/or sexual excitement, competition, self-determination

Existential Questions: What do I value? What is precious to me? What do I find beautiful? What is it worth? What (whom) do I want? What attracts me?

♂ Mars

Principles: Will to action, How one pursues what one wants, vitality, assertion, directness, passion, fight-or-flight, strife.

Drives: To want or desire, to be independent, to have one's own way, to penetrate, to survive, to take action.

Needs: Physical and/or sexual excitement, competition, self-determination.

Existential Questions: What do I want? What can I do? How can I get what (whom) I want? How can I win? What will I fight for? How am I an individual?

♃ Jupiter

Principles: Expansion, judgment, understanding, meaning, pattern recognition, insight, moral values, religion, philosophy, vision, travel.

Drives: To believe or have faith in, to (re)connect to something larger than oneself, to search for meaning, to see the world.

Needs: Faith, trust, meaning, improvement, growth of self, righteousness.

Existential Questions: What do I believe? What is truth? Where am I going? What does it mean? What is good and what is evil? What do I see?

♄ Saturn

Principles: Contraction, purpose, structure, parameters, authority, obligation, duty, responsibility, commitment, restriction, discipline, maturity, efficiency, the right use of resources.

Drives: To crystallize, to build, to learn skills, to conform, to define one's social/vocational role, to administrate, to maintain.

Needs: Social approval, respect, boundaries, structures, stability, skills.

Existential Questions: What are my limitations? What can I learn from them? How do I define this? What is my role in the world? What can, can't and must I do?

♅ Uranus

Principles: Idealization, archival mind, revolution, revelation, liberation, deviation, eccentricity, genius, originality, invention, perversity.

Drives: To be different, to be free, to shock, to liberate, to know.

Needs: Fraternity, liberty, equality, a cause, a structure to rebel against.

Existential Questions: What makes me unique? How am I unusual? What are my ideals? How do I fit into the group/community? Who are those of like mind? What is freedom to me?

♆ Neptune

Principles: Divine Love, universality, compassion, (dis) illusion, confusion, delusion, fusion, deception, mystery, mysticism, perfection, longing, compassion.

Drives: To escape, to experience altered states of consciousness, to surrender, to suffer.

Needs: Oneness with life, dreams, yearnings, longings, connection to the *other* side.

Existential Questions: To be or not to be? What is reality? Can it be trusted? What is greater than I? What should I surrender to? When is beauty the same as truth? Why can't I live there?

♇ Pluto

Principles: Divine force, fate, decay, death, rebirth, regeneration, transformation, transmutation, elimination, catharsis, inevitability of natural cycles.

Drives: To destroy, to shed what is unnecessary, to totally transform, to penetrate to the core of experience, to expose, to bring to light, to drop the persona.

Needs: Purification, surrender of old forms to new ones, shared ecstasy, unconditional acceptance.

Existential Questions: Is there a purpose? Where is my locus of control? What's happening beneath the surface? Who is out to get me? How am I transforming?

Signs

♈

♈
Aries, the Ram,
Ruled by Mars,
Individualization
"I am"
In the body Aries is associated with the head and the adrenal glands.

Warrior	Adventurer	Number One
Crusader	Daredevil	Champion
Pioneer	Leader	Singleton

Ardent	contentious	impatient	original
action-oriented	enthusiastic	forward	head-strong
aggressive	impulsive	independent	inspirational
belligerent	pushy	self-directed	willful.

♉
Taurus, The Bull
Ruled by Venus
Formation
"I have"
In the body Taurus is associated with the jaw, neck and pituitary gland.

builder	self-indulger	singer
sensualist	Immovable rock	miser
bulldozer	owner	materialist

enduring	persevering	retentive	stubborn
loyal	possessive	sensual	thorough
attached	practical	slow	greedy
patient	reliable	steady	indolent

♊
Gemini, The Twins
Ruled by Mercury
Translation
"I think"
In the body Gemini is associated with tubes and pathways, arms/hands and hormones.

Translator	Messenger	Trickster
Reporter	Gossip	Juggler
Round peg/square hole	Wit	Social butterfly

Agile	curious	imitative	moody/depressed
amoral	eloquent	insensitive	
charming	flighty	quick	
clever	glib	scattered	
contradictory	high strung	talkative	

♋
Cancer, The Crab
Ruled by the Moon
Nurturance
"I need"
In the body associated with the stomach, womb and all the containers in the body.

protector	cook	mother
family historian	baby	hoarder
nurturer	patriot	

busy	clannish	emotional	hypersensitive
cautions	consoling	familial	manipulative
maternal	smothering	sulky	
protective		tenacious	

♌
Leo, The Lion
Ruled by the Sun
Emanation
"I Will"
In the body associated with the heart and spine.

Monarch	Entertainer	Big shot
Show-off	Lover of life/children	
Heart of gold	Director	
Shining light	Coward	

arrogant	dramatic	insecure	optimistic
boastful	ego-centric	grandiose	pompous
demanding	flamboyant	loyal	self-indulgent
	fun-loving	noble	warm

♍

Virgo, the Virgin
Ruled by Mercury
Application
"I serve"
In the body associated with the small intestine and the process of assimilation.

	Worrier	Prostitute
	Critic	Servant
	Health fanatic	Medial One
Skeptic	Helper	
Puritan	Nurse/Nun	

aloof	detailed	modest	ritualistic/sexual
analytical	diligent	orderly	skeptical
anxious	sacred space	pragmatic	selective
critiquing	helpful	problem-solving	sub-subservient

♎

Libra, the Scales
Ruled by Venus
Interaction
"I relate"
In the body associated with the kidneys and the process of homeostasis.

Diplomat	Negotiator	Strategist
Pleaser	Pretender	Flirt
See-saw	Competitor	Debater

charming	diplomatic	non-reactive	rational
civilized	indecisive	option-building	sociable
compromising	insincere	oscillating	suave
cultured	mediating	passive-aggressive	

♏

Scorpio, the Scorpion, Snake, Eagle
Ruled by Mars and Pluto
Transformation
"I desire"
In the body associated with the organs of elimination, genitals, sinuses.

Detective	Hypnotist	Shaman
Destroyer	Extremist	Sorcerer
Swamp	Powerhouse	Alchemist

ambitious	mysterious	powerful	secretive
controlling	obsessive	resentful	steadfast
arrogant	perceptive	resourceful	subversive
	possessive	sarcastic	vindictive

♐

Sagittarius, the Archer
Ruled by Jupiter
Revelation
"I see!"
In the body associated with the hips and the liver.

Philosopher	Evangelist	Gypsy
Professor	Gambler	Seeker
Judge	Explorer	Free Spirit

aspiring	didactic	contemptuous	searching
boastful	dogmatic	honest	speculative
careless	freedom-loving	artistic/visionary	tactless
morose	friendly	irresponsible	wise
judgmental	jovial		

♑

Capricorn, the Goat
Ruled by Saturn
Demonstration
"I use."
In the body associated with the joints, bones and skin.

Boss (Manager)	Hermit	Realist
Loner	Denier	Stoic
Administrator	Scapegoat	Control Freak

authoritarian	manipulative	patient	prudent
dedicated	mercenary	pessimistic	rigid
distinguished	organized	practical	serious
efficient	paranoid	professional	

♒

Aquarius, the Water Bearer
Ruled by Saturn and Uranus.
Association
"I know".
In the body associated with the ankles and the process of circulation.

Exile	Politician	Idealist
Genius	Distant one	
Anarchist	Misfit	
Scientist	Heretic	

abstract

cool	original	rebellious	truth-seeking
friendly	principled	resolute	universal/extra-terrestrial
impersonal	progressive	ruthless ideals	
innovative	quirky	social	

♓
Pisces, the Fi sh
Ruled by Jupiter/Neptune.
Absorption
"I believe" ("I am nothing").
In the body associated with the feet and the lymphatic system.

Space Cadet	Mystic	Redeemer
Victim/martyr	Dreamer	Addict
Poet	Escapist	Illusionist

all-giving	hypersensitive	self-pitying
deceptive	impressionable	surrendering
drifting	inspired	thin-skinned
elusive	parasitic	visionary
empathetic	psychic	disillusioned

ASTROLOGICAL AXES KEYWORDS FOR NORTH AND SOUTH NODES:

☊ ☋ Node

Not a planet therefore not subject to principles, drives, needs or existential questions! Simply this: the south node ☋ tells the story of your past, where you come from in a past life or early in this one. What your natural talents and proclivities are. What you must overcome or integrate to achieve your ☊ north node which symbolizes your spiritual evolutionary direction. You are not comfortable in it but you can't stop trying. It's good for your soul but challenging psychologically

♈ **Aries**: I am. Identity. Individuality
♎ **Libra**: I relate. Negotiation. I debate. I seek harmony. The contracts we make.
Together this pair is identity and relationship.

♉ **Taurus**: I have. Sensation. Pleasure. Value.
♏ **Scorpio**: I desire. Initiation. Transformation (whatever it takes). Loss.
Together this pair is mine and yours.

♊ **Gemini**: I think. Communication. Curiosity.
♐ **Sagittarius:** I see. Visionary. Morality. Judgment.
Together this pair is lower and higher mind.

♋ **Cancer**: I feel. I need. Bonding.
♑ **Capricorn**: I use. Stewardship. Management. The right use of resources.
Together this pair is about security and responsibility.

♌ **Leo**: I will. Spontaneity. Creativity. Divine right.
♒ **Aquarius:** I know. Hopes and fears. Like minded people. idealism, idea-ism, humanitarian, friendly.
Together this pair is about heart and mind.

♍ **Virgo**: I analyze. I adjust. I integrate. Order makes meaning. Seeking meaning in the mundane.
♓ **Pisces**: I believe (without proof.) Longing. Yearning. Mysticism. Make me One with Everything.
Together this pair is about service: practical and selfless.

The Houses

The First House
Appearance, how others see you, personality, the physical body, general constitution, first impression on others, birth experience, the mask that you wear, formative influences, how you interface with the world.

The Second House
What you value, self-worth, personal resources, finances, spending habits, money, physical sense of the body, attachments, possessions, pleasure.

The Third House
Communication, routine functioning of the mind, intellectual endeavor, writing, teaching, the local neighborhood, siblings, elementary school.

The Fourth House
Where you belong, home (childhood or adult), roots, heritage, family traditions, one parent (usually father), foundations, real estate, security, the tribe, family of origin.

The Fifth House
Where you have fun, love affairs, creativity, children, amusements, hobbies, entertainment, gambling, speculative investments, acting and role playing.

The Sixth House

Where you prepare, service, work environment, employment, employees, health, and health care, lifestyle, habits, personal refinement, details of life, hygiene, routines, rituals, rites of passage.

The Seventh House

Projection onto others, relationship, what you seek from others, marriage, one-to-one interactions, partnerships, open enemies, contracts, lawsuits, counseling relationships, cooperation or competition, what you learned from your parents about marriage.

The Eighth House

Where you share, where you transform, the power dynamics of relationship, who has control over you, partner's resources and values, death, sexual intimacy, taxes, the occult, legacies, wills, inheritance, psychotherapy, secrets.

The Ninth House

Where you worship, the search for truth, meaning and faith, long trips, religion, philosophy, foreign influences and involvement, higher education, wisdom, ideology, ethics, morals, teachers.

The Tenth House

Goals, what you aspire to or build, profession, career, the public self (reputation and social standing), the mark you make, vocation, authority figures, social role, the other parent (usually mother).

The Eleventh House

Where one reaches out and establishes contacts with the group, friends and social circle, people of like mind, social or political groups, professional colleagues, social causes and ideals, hopes and wishes for the future, financial investments

The Twelfth House

Where you go to be alone, asylums, ashrams, institutions, hospitals, secret enemies, past lives, the unconscious, ego transcendence, sacrifice, spiritual connection, hidden aspects of your life, family secrets.

Ascendant Key Words

Each description is a key phrase to suggest the primary survival instinct for each rising sign. Pick the one that seems to describe you most accurately but don't be afraid to change if suddenly another one seems to fit better.

Aries: I survive because I am a fighter and highly individualistic.

Taurus: I survive because I hold on and I know what I want.

Gemini: I survive because I can think fast and use my wits.

Cancer: I survive because I feel my needs as well as the needs of others.

Leo: I survive because I am strong in many ways and proud.

Virgo: I survive because I figure things out fast and I'm helpful.

Libra: I survive because I always see the other option and I am willing to fight for peace.

Scorpio: I survive because I can manipulate whatever it takes and I feel what is true in my gut.

Sagittarius: I survive because I have faith and keep moving.

Capricorn: I survive because I do the responsible thing and I can manage no matter what.

Aquarius: I survive because I live up to my ideals and I have lots of friends.

Pisces: I am not sure how I survive or even that I have survived.

**Here is a very subjective and terribly general description of things that could help you decide what your ascendant might be:

Aries *rising* people look fierce and warrior-like, although they may be very nice. They can be fierce and in your face like rams or timid and sweet like lambs. Either way they are constantly trying to define their individuality.

Taurus *rising* people look comfortable as if you could sidle up to them and be safe. But if you get close to them you can see they are often bottled up inside. They are sweet and easy going unless and until they see the red flag at which time they become the bull!

Gemini *rising* people often gesticulate with their hands and they tend to be restless and talk a lot. They are plagued by their reflexive need to change the channels of life. Distraction is their enemy, humor is their gift and gossip their pitfall.

Cancer *rising* people are hidden from view. Often their eyes are a bit protected by their eyebrows. They want security but they also can be bossy because they know what's good for everyone.

Leo *rising* people are magnetic; beautiful or not they attract others. They like to dress well if they are happy. If they are sad they can hid their light under the bushel better than anyone.

Virgo *rising* people have fine or perfect features in some way. They are very analytical which often means that even if they are beautiful it never is good enough for them! They tend toward self criticism. They may look younger than they are. They can have bad skin. Acne or something like that.

Libra *rising* people are graceful and go out of their way to make sure they have been reasonable with people. They like to debate and are often in the dark about how it is they started the argument.

Scorpio *rising* people look intense. Their eyes can be deep set in a kind of darkness. If they are under a dark cloud you know it. Even so they may put an unreasonable amount of energy into trying to be nice. They can feel guilty and blaming in the same moment. They are exceptionally perceptive.

Sagittarius *rising* people are the kind that like to travel in mind or body. There is often something about them that looks horsy. They gravitate toward situations that can teach them something.

Capricorn *rising* people are solid. You can often see this in the sturdy bone structure of their head. They can often eat just about anything. They will try to manage the situation even as they tell you they don't want any more responsibility.

Aquarius *rising* people are often curly-haired and cuddly. They need friends but even so they often feel that they don't fit in. They are high-minded and don't understand how people can act so badly sometimes.

Pisces *rising* people have difficulty sticking with their center of gravity. You can see this in the way they walk. It is often hard to remember exactly how they look when you are not with them. They can have an amazing sense of humor. They are insightful about others but often can't see clearly about themselves at all.

The Eight Phases of the Moon

Each phase of the moon is listed with some of its positive traits or challenges as well as some of its more negative traits after the word 'without'.

New

The *challenge* is to be present in the moment, spontaneous and alive *without* demanding all the attention or succumbing to over stimulation.

Crescent

The *challenge* is to work hard at something for the sake of doing it, to follow this impulse wherever it may lead *without* oversimplification, conformity, or excessive solitary reflection.

First Quarter

The *challenge* is to strengthen the will; to be strong and passionate; find strength in defeat and be willing to sail into the wind of conflict if necessary *without* selling out to authority, blaming others for your situation, and/or blundering and chaotic emotional behavior.

Gibbous

The *challenge* is to be faithful to your personal destiny; discover, organize and express your inner truth—just because—*without* succumbing to flattery, excessive advice from external sources and/or self-absorption.

Full

The *challenge* is to see yourself in all experiences and relationships knowing that all of life is reflection; to overcome disillusionment while staying connected to close companions; idealistic *without* judgment, loneliness, alienation and quixotic idealism.

Disseminating

The *challenge* is to master life with the mind; to share your ideas with dramatic conviction and creative delivery *without* fanaticism or trying to control the minds of others; cruelty to self and/or others; misuse of power.

Third Quarter

The *challenge* is to rise to positions of responsibility, using the status quo as it stands without doing it for your personal ambition; to make a difference in life *without* conforming to who people think you are; being naive or being fearful of taking charge.

Balsamic

The *challenge* is to accept life as it is; to cultivate penetrating insights and make the most of each moment; to let awareness of death intensify life *without* pride, over identification with individuality, ambition, obsessive purification or poisonous rage.

Astrology Tables

If you would like the specific location of the planets we use in this book as well as the moon phase and ascendant you can send $15.00 Canadian or US to: Julie Simmons 1562 Danforth Ave., P.O. Box 72089 Toronto, ON, Canada M4J 5C1

Sun Sign Dates

The following dates are for when the Sun is said to be in each sign of the zodiac. They vary slightly from year to year but are always within a day of these dates. We call this the cusp. If you were born at a cusp you might consider whether you are at the end of the last sign (and live a life that is constantly on the edge) or at the beginning of the next sign (and life a life of endlessly discovering that things are not exactly what you thought). As a person on the cusp you can do both/and rather than either/or.

Aries: March 20 to April 18
Taurus: April 19 to May 19
Gemini: May 20 to June 19
Cancer: June 20 to July 21
Leo: July 22 to August 21
Virgo: August 22 to September 21
Libra: September 22 to October 21
Scorpio: October 22 to November 20
Sagittarius: November 21 to December 21
Capricorn: December 22 to January 19
Aquarius: January 20 to February 18
Pisces: February 19 to March 19

Chiron for people born 1935-1960

(Note: For greater accuracy, consult an astrologer or have your natal chart calculated. Because planets have retrograde motion the dates on the cusps are not totally accurate.)

Chiron in Gemini: January 1935 to August 1937
Chiron in Cancer: September 1937 to November 1937
Chiron in Gemini: December 1937 to May 1938
Chiron in Cancer: June 1938 to June 1941
Chiron in Leo: July 1941-July 1943
Chiron in Virgo: August 1943-July 1945
Chiron in Libra: August 1945-November 1946
Chiron in Scorpio: December 1946-November 1948
Chiron in Sagittarius: December 1948-November 1951
Chiron in Capricorn: December 1951-January 1955
Chiron in Aquarius: February 1955-January 1961

Pluto

Pluto in Cancer: January 1, 1935 to September 1937
Pluto in Leo: October 1937 to November 1937
Pluto in Cancer: December 1937 to July 1938
Pluto in Leo: August 1938 to January 1939
Pluto in Cancer: February 1939 to May 1939
Pluto in Leo: June 1939 to August 1957
Pluto in Virgo: August 1957-September 1971

Neptune

Neptune in Virgo: January 1935 to July 1943
Neptune in Libra: August 1943-October 1956
Neptune in Scorpio: November 1956-October 1970

Uranus

Uranus in Aries: January 1935 to March 1935
Uranus in Taurus: April 1935 to July 1941
Uranus in Gemini: August 1941-May 1949
Uranus in Cancer: June 1949-August 1955
Uranus in Leo: September 1955-August 1962

Nodes: Change signs in a little more than a year.
Saturn: Changes signs every two and a half years.
Jupiter: Changes signs in about a year.

The return of Saturn and Jupiter to the original sign and house they were in at birth happens only once in sixty years. In the general cycle of the transits of planets through the heavens, this conjunction occurs every twenty years in different signs.

Appendix II

Exercises

EXERCISES FOR CHAPTER 2: LAYING THE GROUNDWORK

Chiron Exercise

Part 1: Find the astrological placement of Chiron in your chart. (Refer to Appendix I.)

Your date of birth determines what sign Chiron is in, but you will only know for certain what house Chiron is in if you also have the time of your birth. You may use the simple keyword list in Appendix I for inspiration. If you do not have the time of your birth simply choose the keyword that seems most descriptive for you at this time. Create a sentence using the following structure: *The wounds that have not healed in me come from a time when . . .*

Esther's Chiron is in Gemini in her 12th house.

Gemini is about communication as well as siblings. The 12th house is about being alone, possibly alienated or, if you have done the work, spiritually connected. Esther's sentence is: *The wounds that have not healed in me come from a time when I felt all alone in trying to understand what was going on between me and my brother.*

Linda has Chiron in Scorpio in her first house. Scorpio is a sign of transformation that often comes through loss. The first house is the personality. Linda's sentence is: *The wounds that haven't healed in me come from a time when the pain of betrayal turned inside me to a desire for revenge.*

Kate has Chiron in Aquarius in her third house. Aquarius is a sign of possibilities and aspirations. The second house is about value and self worth. Kate's sentence is: *The wounds that haven't healed in me seem to be about never having accomplished enough.*

Part 2: Now put your keyword sentence aside. It has done its work by stimulating the subconscious. Write for ten minutes without stopping on the topic of "Wisdom Gained: How the wounds that haven't healed have been and continue to be my teachers."

MOON RETURN EXERCISE

Because the Moon changes sign every two and a half days it is not possible to offer a chart in this book which can tell you what sign the Moon was in when you were born. If you don't have a birth chart, simply choose the placement of the Moon that seems to fit at the moment you are doing the exercise and be assured that it will help you find your way to the right information.

Make a keyword sentence for your Moon by sign and house. Refer to the keywords in Appendix I. Use the following sentence as the place to begin: *I need to be* (refer to the sign placement for the Moon in your natal chart) *in the realm of* (refer to the house placement of the Moon in your natal chart) *to feel that I am getting my needs met.*

Do not be concerned if the structuring of this sentence seems awkward. The goal is simply to activate the issues.

Esther's Moon is in Virgo which is about precision, analytical ability and perfectionism. It is in the third house which is about rudimentary learning as well as who our siblings are. Her sentence is: *I endlessly strive for perfection in everything that I study.* She also felt inclined to add a second sentence which is: *I need to analyze and understand my relationship with my brother if I am ever to have any peace.*

In Linda's chart the Moon is in Aquarius, which is about knowledge or understanding. It is located in her fourth house, which represents the family of origin. Linda played with these keywords for a bit and came up with this sentence: *I need to understand the dynamics of my family to feel even remotely comfortable.*

Kate's Moon sign is Libra suggesting themes of cooperation and competition as well as fairness and justice. It is in the ninth house which is the place of higher learning, vision and moral perspective. Her sentence is: *I need to strive and do the very best I can to feel comfortable with myself.*

Next, look back to the time when you were between 25 and 27. See if there is a connection between what was happening then and your keyword sentence.

Having made a keyword sentence for your own Moon's sign and house, put it aside and write for ten minutes without stopping on the subject of: *What am I like when I am needy? Who meets those needs for me? How well or badly do they meet them? How do I meet them for myself?*

EXERCISES FOR CHAPTER 3: HOLY SPARKS

Forgiveness and restorative love.

Think back to a time when someone you trusted and loved hurt you. It is possible that the person who hurt you was yourself. As you think on these events don't be afraid to let feelings from that time come to the surface. You are conjuring the past. When you have done this for a few minutes write for ten minutes, without stopping, about the person or people you need to forgive and what you need to forgive them for.

Alternatively: If your memory falls in the category of irresolvable traumatic events do not bother with forgiveness for the other or yourself write instead on the theme of restorative love. What would it mean to restore love to yourself in the face of traumatic experiences from your past?

When you are done, write for five more minutes on how forgiveness and/or restorative love could free your spirit, creating "holy sparks" and raising you to a higher level of awareness. What might it feel like to be at peace with the negative feelings from the past and how might these feelings touch your world?

Your Generation

Write for ten minutes on the gap between your generation and your parents' generation and how this affected you.

Write for ten more minutes on how being part of your generation has influenced your life.

Your Ascendant, or Rising Sign

If you have a copy of your chart your Ascendant is the same as the sign on the cusp of your first house. Go directly to the keyword sheet for the signs (Appendix I). If you don't have your birth chart simply choose the keywords that seem to most accurately capture a significant quality of your personality. In either case, using your chosen keywords for the sign which is indicated by your Ascendant or most accurately reflects your personality make a simple sentence for yourself which begins, *I know who I am when* (fill in the keywords for the sign). Then make another sentence which begins, *When I am defensive I tend to* (fill in the keywords for the sign).

Esther is a Cancer rising. Her sentences are: *I know who I am when I feel strongly that I must act on my feelings. When I am defensive I tend to try to make myself comfortable by taking care of the people around me.*

Linda is a Libra rising. Her sentences are: *I know who I am when I am compelled to stand up for justice and fairness. When I am defensive I start a debate about whatever it is that makes me feel defensive.*

Kate is a Capricorn rising. Her sentences are: *I know who I am when I am taking responsibility for whatever is happening. When I am defensive I go into overdrive and manage everyone and everything in sight. I know that I am the only one who can get it right.*

Writing exercise: After you have written your sentences, put them aside and write for ten minutes—without thinking it through beforehand—on the topic of: *How my survival instinct has become my persona.*

EXERCISES FOR CHAPTER FOUR: THE HEART'S DESIRE

The Sun

Think back to your relationship with your father. Start with your first awareness of him. Looking at photos of him from when you were a child can help to jog your memory. Do a mental review of your perception of your father as well as the relationship between the two of you until you reached the age of 18.

When you have completed this, write for ten minutes on: *What I learned from my father about taking risks.*

Now find the Sun in your chart and determine the sign and house that it is in. Make a sentence using the keywords. *I am proud to express {Sign} in {House}.*

Remember that keywords unlock the path to understanding a symbol, not a specific meaning itself. The keyword sentences that you create aren't meant to express everything about you. They simply help to unlock your ability to see something about yourself at a deeper level than before.

Esther has the Sun in the 2nd house in Leo. Her sentence is: *I am proud to express my Self through my values.* Linda has the Sun in Taurus in the 8th house. Her sentence is: *I am proud that my ability to see deeply into other people helps them to transform.* Kate has the Sun in Scorpio in the 10th house. Her sentence is: *I am proud to be the master of my responsibilities.*

Once you have created your keyword sentence for the Sun, consider how it is fundamentally different from the sentence you created for your Ascendant in Chapter 3. The Ascendant is easily crystallized into over-identification because it often experiences fear. The Sun is the path of liberation. It is meant to encourage us to take risks and be the most we can be.

A special consideration: Some people, if they were born around the time of sunrise will have the Sun and the Ascendant in the same sign. This is just one of the myriad of combinations that astrology offers. The way to work with it is to realize that the sign you are dealing with has one side that is fear based, a way of behaving that defends it from danger (the Ascendant), and another side that suggests the path of true, heart-felt accomplishment (the Sun). If this is your situation write for five minutes on *the difference between fear and love.*

Once you have teased these ideas into some kind of froth put the keywords aside and write for 10 minutes on: *False pride that keeps me prisoner vs. true pride that sets me free.*

EXERCISES FOR JUPITER

Without considering your astrological Jupiter at the moment write for five minutes on *the prevailing belief system of the community of which I was a part when I was twelve and how it affected me.*

Now, using the keywords make a sentence that takes into account the sign and house placement for your Jupiter. *I believe (sign) and I demonstrate my beliefs (house).* If you do not know the house placement of your Jupiter simply choose the one that most resonates with where in your life you tend to express your beliefs.

Esther has Jupiter in Sagittarius in the 5th house but close to the 6th. Her sentence is, *I believe that it is important to seek out the truth about health and daily habits. I believe that this is what has helped me beat my illness back.*

Linda has Jupiter in Scorpio in the 2nd house. Her sentence is, *I believe in the necessity of constantly questioning my choices. I believe that by listening deeply for the messages people give me about their values I can help them transform their lives.*

Kate has Jupiter in Capricorn in the twelfth house. Her sentence is, *I believe in doing things the right way and I demonstrate this by devoting myself to working as hard as I need to for the benefit of the success of whatever I am working on.*

Once you have made your sentence see if you can find a common thread that connects how your vision today relates to ones you might have had at twelve, 24, 36, and 48. Make a list for each age and some notes about what was going on for you in terms of education, travel or legal or religious matters. Once you have some sense of a common thread consider how you might benefit from being less certain and more able to live with paradox and ambiguity where your beliefs are concerned.

Write for ten minutes on the topic of: *What I believe is possible . . .*

EXERCISES FOR CHAPTER 5: BODY AND SOUL

For this chapter you need a photograph of yourself when you were somewhere between 25 and 32 as well as a recent photo. It would also be helpful to have a photograph of someone who was old when you were young that you loved and revered.

Moon Phase

Once you have figured out which Moon phase resonates with you (see Appendix I), do the following exercises: (Remember that if you don't actually know which Moon phase you were born under just choose the one that feels most right.)

The Moon Phase description includes both a positive and a negative statement.

1. Write for ten minutes on what you recognize about yourself from the description of your Moon Phase.
2. Write for ten minutes on how the relationship issues of your late twenties are reflected in the relationship issues of your late fifties. (If you aren't that old yet, project yourself into the near future. If you have passed your 50s simply relate you past relationship issues to your life at the moment.)

When you are done, take out the photos of yourself in your late twenties and the one of you now. Look at the earlier photo of yourself. If you are doing this process with friends, pass your photos around for one another to see. Comments and exclamations are welcome!

For the next part, you can either write if you are by yourself or talk if you are in a group. Start with a predominantly physical description of the person you see in the photo.

When you are done, take a moment to close your eyes and rest inside yourself. Breathe. Relax. Scan your body from head to toe.

Now open your eyes and look at the photo of yourself in the present.

Speak or write a predominantly physical description of the person you see in this photo.

When you are done, take another moment to close your eyes and rest inside yourself. Breathe. Relax. Scan your body from head to toe, exactly the way you did after describing the first photo.

When you feel deeply relaxed, touch your face with your fingers. Outline the shape of it, feel the texture of the skin. Trace your eyes, nose and mouth as you stay with your inner sense of things. Include the jaw and the neck. Keep your eyes closed.

When you are done, open your eyes and without moving or distracting yourself, write for ten minutes on: "As I age I see myself changing physically . . ."

Take a break.

Now look at the photo of the old person that you chose. Write for ten minutes on the beauty that you see in this person's photo. And the beauty of the feelings you remember when you were together.

Who do you see when you look in the mirror? Which parent do you favor physically?

Write for ten minutes on which parent you see in the mirror and how you feel about that.

Esther was born at the New Moon. Linda was born at the Disseminating Moon Phase. Kate was born at the Balsamic Moon Phase.

Venus

Find Venus in your chart by house and by sign. If you do not have access to this information simply choose the keywords that seem to fit for you. Make a sentence for this planet using the most essential Venus statement: "I love (fill in the blank using the keywords for the house and sign of your Venus)."

Esther's Venus is in Virgo in the 3rd house. Her sentence is *"I love precision in communication. I love it especially when I play music and when I work with the body."*

Linda's Venus is in Aries in the 7th house. Her sentence is *I love the challenge which relationships offer and how that makes me more aware of myself.*

Kate's Venus is in Capricorn in the 12th house. Her sentence is *I love to take charge and manage things in such a way that people aren't even aware that I have done it. I love to be part of the underlying structure of things.*

Once again take out the photo of yourself when you were in your late twenties. Let us imagine that this is a photo of Psyche—young, beautiful and possibly an outrage or at least a difficulty for the part of you that is growing old. You are Venus herself, immortal goddess of Love, assaulted by these conflicting emotions that arise because you are being usurped by a mere girl who is doomed to die! This is your older, possibly somewhat bitter self talking to your younger, ignorant, innocent, beautiful self.

Leave the photo where you can see it.

Write for five minutes or more on the following question: *What did your young, beautiful self need to sort out about love and beauty?*

Write for five minutes or more on *moments in my adult life when relinquishing the fierce and dangerous defense mechanisms of my personality allowed me to harvest gold.*

Write for five minutes or more on *how it was for the young woman in your photo when she had to face powerful feelings that tumbled and fell inside her on account of the loss of something she wanted or someone she loved? What has she learned from loss?*

Write for five minutes or more on *what tender mercy you have experienced in your adult life that could allow you to embrace and experience beauty in your elder years? Will your inner Psyche find it in the mirror or somewhere else?*

The Love Affair

This exercise may take you a day or a week, even a month or more. Take your time doing it and use all the source material that your life offers, especially that which you have unearthed in the above exercises.

Write a poem or a short-story; make a drawing or a painting; create a piece of music or a song that expresses the relationship between your body/mind and your soul. It may not be all sweetness and light. It doesn't have to be all misery and angst. You are honoring a relationship here; there is always room for paradox and ambiguity, especially at this stage of our lives.

The Nodes

Nodes are not actually heavenly bodies. They are points in space determined by combining the movements of the Sun with the movement of any other heavenly body. The Moon's Nodes are determined by looking for the points in space where the apparent path of the Sun around the Earth intersects with the apparent path of the Moon. They are created by making two big circles describing these movements and marking the points where they intersect. Because the Sun and the Moon are the brightest lights in the sky (known as the luminaries) they are symbolically the most powerful. At the time of an eclipse of either the Sun or the Moon it is as if these life giving lights are being devoured. Because the Nodes are always close to the Sun and Moon during an eclipse they are considered to be the devouring monster. Down through the ages the Sun and the Moon have generated much symbolic information for us. These Nodal points have been considered to be very important for a long time.

Here's an exercise you can do to see how the Nodes function in your life. Find your North and South Node by sign and by house position. If you have an astrological chart that only gives you the North Node you can determine your South node because it will be in the exact opposite sign and house. If you do not have access to your horoscope you may not know which houses your nodes fall in. Simply choose the one that seems to fit best. Refer to 'Appendix I: Nodes' for keywords for signs and houses to determine the essence of your sentences. The keywords for how signs work in opposite pairs is specifically useful for working with the Nodes given that they are always exactly opposite each other. They are always in opposing signs and houses. Opposites seem to both repel and attract.

Make two keyword sentences, one for the South Node and one for the North as follows:

The sentence for the South Node goes something like this: "I have a habitual attitude of (sign) that I feel compelled to express in (house)."

The sentence for the North Node goes something like this: "I believe my growing edge is about (sign) and I must learn to use it when I am in (house)."

Esther's North Node is in Capricorn in the 6th house and her South Node is therefore in Cancer in the 12th house. Her South Node sentence is: *"I have a habitual attitude of feeling things deeply and keeping them to myself."* Her North Node sentence is: *"My growing edge is about taking responsibility for healing myself."*

Linda's North Node is in Gemini in the 8th and therefore her South Node is in Sagittarius in the 2nd. Her South Node sentence is: *"I have a habit of judging people based on their values."* Her North Node sentence is: *"I believe my growing edge is about being a non-judgmental listener—a witness—to what people tell me, which then helps them to transform."*

Kate's North Node is in Virgo in the 8th house and therefore her South Node is in Pisces in the 2nd house. Her South Node sentence is: *"I have a habit of offering myself and my resources in a big way to the task at hand."* Her North Node sentence is: *"I feel my growing edge when I allow myself to accept transformation and let it change me even if I haven't ordained it and can't control it."*

Read over your South and North Node sentences. Put them aside and write for ten minutes on *how my habitual responses hold me back and what challenges me to try something else.*

When you are done with that, take a break and when you return write for ten more minutes on *how I would be if I was not controlled by my unconscious patterns from the past.*

EXERCISES FOR CHAPTER 6: RESPONSIBILITY

Saturn

Part 1: Write for five minutes on: *Who showed you the ropes? Who taught you to eat your vegetables and how to use the toilet? Who demonstrated over and over again that the stove and the iron can be hot?*

Without deliberation, write down the first example that comes into your head upon reading the following sentence: How is it that great (or small) difficulties in childhood turned into a skill (even a negative one) in adulthood around the age of 29 (which is your first Saturn Return). (Example: if you lost a parent early in your life, did you become an adult who is lonely and depressed or someone who tries to help people suffering from early loss? Or both!)

Read over what you have just written. Now consider how this skill has served and/or blocked you as an adult and write out your thoughts for ten minutes.

When you are done, put these two pieces of writing aside as if they are one. You will return to them later.

Write for another 10 minutes: *How might you best use this quality or skill in your elder years?*

Part 2: All these things that we have been discussing are related to the Saturn principle. Now it is time to find your very own Saturn and see what particular information it might have to offer.

Locate the sign and house placement of your Saturn. (For this you will need a copy of your chart.) If you do not have the time of your birth you cannot know which house Saturn falls in. Simply choose the one that seems to fit best for you.

Make a keyword sentence as follows: *I respond (sign) to my (house).*

Esther has Saturn in Pisces in the 9th house. Her sentence is: *I respond with intense feeling to my beliefs.*

Linda has Saturn in Leo in the 10th house. Her sentence is: *I work very hard and believe I should be an example to others in my profession.*

Kate has Saturn in Capricorn in the 1st house. Her sentence is: *I manage myself that I may achieve my goals, be they personal or professional.*

Part 3: Once you have completed the exercise for your own Saturn you can do an extra exercise if you have a child or a parent who was born with Saturn in the same sign as you have it. You would have to be born approximately 28 or 29 years apart.

Write for ten minutes about how your transitions into a different stage of life are similar to or different from the parent or child who is twenty-eight years older or younger than you. You could also skip the writing and, if they are willing, just talk to them about the connection you have, using the theme of Saturn by sign as the starting point.

Part 4: A common way to imagine Saturn is as the keeper of the gate. Saturn marks the threshold and as the planet that symbolizes the notion that there are consequences to our actions it represents the energy that challenges us as we make transitions in life. Once you have found your Saturn sentence you might do the following visualization. A good way to set it up if you have no one to read it to you is to record it first and then follow the images as if someone else is telling it to you. Feel free to embellish it according to your own preferences.

Make yourself comfortable and get into your personal visualization mode. Breathe, relax and center. Once you feel quiet and your body and breath have stilled, imagine that you are going down. You may go down steps or walk a winding path that clearly descends. However you imagine yourself going down is fine. Perhaps you have a familiar place where you look for the kind of truth you can't see above ground; where time is non-existent and space has its own reality. Go there now. When you get to the bottom look around for the gate. When you locate it take a moment to study it well. Is it simple or ornate? Is it large or small? What does it feel like if you touch it? As you perceive this gate you will find the keeper of the gate who stands near it. Does s/he stand before it, beside it, above it? Take notice of this. At this time there is no need to make contact unless you feel moved to. It is simply enough to observe this being with as many of your senses as you can. How does it smell? What color is it? What shape? Is there a sound that emanates from it? Does it speak to you? Can you touch it? Observe it well. When you have had enough and you feel ready, turn away from the gate and the gate keeper and find your stairs, your path to the upper world. Slowly and deliberately, taking one step at a time, return yourself to the upper world. When you have accomplished this take a moment to sit and recall what you have experienced. Then open your eyes and write it down.

Part 5: Take as much time as you need to consider what you would like to receive as an award for completing the adult stage of development. It is as if you are retiring not from your job but from the perspective of adult life. This is the reward you would like to get for your contribution to upholding the status quo for the last twenty-eight-odd years. Use your imagination and don't hold back.

Before you go on to the next part, take a break. It could be fifteen minutes or a day or two. Don't come back to this next part till you feel fresh and ready.

Part 6: Gather up all the things you have written or created since you began the process of reflecting and exploring your elderhood. This includes all the exercises as well as journal entries, dreams and observations you have made since you first started reading this book. Read over what you have written.

Now you will do a few short writing exercises. Don't worry about having the right piece of information in the right category—you can't actually make a mistake.

Write for ten minutes about *your regrets* as discussed in Chapter 6.

Write for ten minutes about *your accomplishments* as discussed in Chapter 6.

Write for ten minutes on *the road ahead.*

- What would you like to do and how would you like to live in this world as an elder, knowing what you do about your regrets and your accomplishments?
- How do you want to use what you have learned from your regrets as well as your accomplishments to make the world the kind of place in which people would want to grow older?
- How might you generate the desire to become an elder in someone younger than you?

At this time it would be useful to take another break and let these things settle. Take a walk, have a cup of tea or put this away until tomorrow or next week.

Part 7: Reread what you have written about your regrets, accomplishments and the road ahead. Take these things that you have recently written and anything else you would like to include and turn it into an acceptance speech. Imagine that you are to be presented with the award of your choice and you must therefore prepare this acceptance speech. It will include what you can do, what you can't do, and what you must do. Or we could say:

- Your regrets (what you can't or didn't do).
- Your accomplishments (what you can and did do).
- The road ahead (what you must do).

Your speech will take into account the principles we have explored thus far, including your heart's desire, your basic emotional nature, your karmic tasks, your fundamental beliefs about life, your basic personality type and, of course, your ability to respond. It is meant to support your position on this planet as an elder. Saturn is about your profession—what you profess to be. How you walk your talk. Convince your audience and yourself that you deserve this award by presenting an acceptance speech for the award of adult life and tell them how you will use this as an elder.

You can go back over what you have written thus far or you can start from scratch. In any case by the time you have done the above exercises you will have stirred your mind up in a way that will have you thinking about all the different things that have contributed to your life as it was, is and will be. [Feel free to visit my website: www.juliesimmons.ca and search out the EARNED WISDOM page to see contributions from other elders].

Creating this presentation can take while: a day, a week, even a month. Once you have written it you need to present it. If you have been doing this work with a group of people, you can be creative with how you make the presentation. You might create a space that looks like a boardroom. Put the chairs in rows, not in a circle. Create a space at the front of the room that looks like a podium. As each person presents her speech another person should be ready with a certificate of your own creation which symbolizes and describes the award that she requested. Dress as if you were at a business meeting. Imagine you are retiring from adult life and entering elderhood. Your acceptance speech acknowledges this in a worldly sense.

If you are doing these exercises on your own it would be good if, for this exercise you could have a friend or family member listen to your presentation. They may or may not understand the full implication of what you are doing, but having them sit before you while you stand and read your piece will create the right effect within yourself.

EXERCISES FOR CHAPTER 7: THRESHOLD: CHAOS, CRISIS, CHANGE

Uranus

Part 1: Whether you have your complete astrological data or not you can know which sign Uranus was in on the day you were born (Appendix I). If you do not have the time of your birth you will have to decide for yourself which house you think Uranus might be in. Using the keywords in Appendix I for the placement of Uranus in your chart by sign and by house make a keyword sentence using the following template: *The chaos that I encounter when [use keywords for the sign and house which Uranus is in to finish this part of the sentence] brings change [of what kind].* Keep in mind as you are fashioning your sentence that chaos is a necessary part of life when change is in the wind. Refer back to this as you do the other exercises for this chapter.

Esther has Uranus in Taurus in the 11th house. Her sentence is: "*The chaos that I encounter when I make choices that are not guided by my ideals brings change in that it reminds me that my ideals are not static. I must constantly investigate the world if I am to keep my ideals relevant and vital to my life.*"

Linda has Uranus in Gemini in the 9th house. Her sentence is: "*The chaos that I encounter when I get overwhelmed by too much information or communication brings change in that it creates a mental anxiety that reminds me that I must practice mindfulness all the time, not just some of the time. It helps me to set priorities as to what I want to spend my time thinking or talking about.*"

Kate has Uranus in Leo in the 8th house. Her sentence is: "*The chaos that I encounter when I feel manipulated by people or events I cannot control or master forces me to change in that it reminds me that there is too much effort in control. When I remember to surrender to what is actually in front of me, it's all so much easier.*"

Part 2: Write for 5 minutes on the similarities and differences between revolution and revelation.

Write for 10 minutes about how the revolutionary impulses of your early 20s relate to possible revelations about yourself and the world around you that you could have or already have had in your 60s and 70s.

Part 3: Uranus often is associated with technology. Write for 10 minutes about when you first got hooked up to the Internet and started using email. Include some thoughts about your life pre and post e-mail.

Part 4: Write and/or rant for 10 minutes on the double messages that create anxiety for you.

Part 5: Write for as long as you want about what you see when you look into the future.

EXERCISES FOR CHAPTER 8: THE PATH LESS TRAVELED

Whether you are on the verge of becoming an elder or you have been an elder for some time, you could create a ritual for yourself that acknowledges crossing the threshold and entering this period in your life. You might have a celebration, inviting those people whose recognition of you as an elder would mean something to you. Celebrate the way our ancestors did: gather people together, offer food and music, good conversation, dance and make merry. Another possibility would be to create an actual ritual. Although many books are written on this subject, I suggest a classic: *The Spiral Dance* by Starhawk (See resources at the end of this book). For this you will need imagination and a willing spirit. The essential requirement of a ritual is to create a circle that places you between this world and the other. The circle you create in a ritual is a threshold in and of itself. Next it is common to invoke the powers of the four directions. East is air, dawn, spring and childhood. South is fire, noon, summer and youth. West is sunset, autumn and adult life. North is earth, midnight, winter, elderhood and beyond. North is the direction of the ancestors, all the ones who have gone before us into the realm of eternity. (If you have a different tradition wherein the directions are associated with different times of day or year it is fine to use that. There is and never will be, one way to create ritual space.)

Once you have created a circle for yourself it is up to you how you would like to honor the threshold. You can do this ritual alone or invite friends to participate or witness your journey. You might read aloud some of the things you have written as you worked through the exercises in this book, for example. It is fine to develop and edit any of the writing exercises to suit your purpose. Once you have accomplished your goals within the circle, it is important at the end of the ritual to open the circle. Thank the energies you have drawn into your circle. Release the four directions, one at a time. And know that you can create this circle for yourself again and again, any time you feel the need, just by calling in the directions.

Notes

Introduction

1. You can read more about this in Chapter 13 of *Sex, Time and Power: How Women's Sexuality Shaped Human Evolution* by Leonard Shlain (New York: Viking Penguin, 2003).
2. Richard Tarnas, *Cosmos and Psyche: Intimations of a New World View* (New York: Viking Penguin, 2006), p. 57.
3. Max Müller, "The Philosophy of Mythology," quoted by Ernst Cassirer in "The Validity and Form of Mythical Thought" in *The Modern Tradition: Backgrounds of Modern Literature,* edited by Richard Ellmann and Charles Feidelson (Oxford: Oxford University Press, 1965), p. 635.
4. *The Hero with a Thousand Faces* by Joseph Campbell (New York: Pantheon, 1949), p. 3.
5. James Hillman, *A Terrible Love of War* (New York: Penguin, 2004), pp. 179-180.
6. The generally accepted birth date for the United States is July 4, 1776 at 5:10 PM LMT Philadelphia, Pennsylvania. According to this chart the Ascendant of the United States is 12 degrees of Sagittarius and the descendant is exactly opposite that point at 12 degrees of Gemini. The Ascendant symbolizes the identity of the country, and the Descendant represents the challengers. On September 11, 2001, Pluto was at 12 degrees of Sagittarius and Saturn was at 14 degrees of Gemini.
7. Tarnas, *Cosmos and Psyche,* p. 209.

8. The astrology used in this book is tropical astrology, the type of astrology most commonly used by Western astrologers.

Chapter 2: Laying the Groundwork

1. Sir William Smith, *Smaller Classical Dictionary* (New York: Dutton, 1958).
2. Coleridge, Samuel Taylor, "The Rime of the Ancient Mariner (1798). This poem is truly a Chironic offering. The Ancient Mariner is compelled to tell his tale which has to do with his gratuitous killing of the albatross and the bad luck that follows his act. He is not finished his tale until he also offers up the wisdom of his suffering which he also wants the listener to take to heart.
3. China Galland, *The Bond Between Women: A Journey to Fierce Compassion* (New York: Riverhead/Penguin, 1998), p. xiv.
4. Ibid.
5. Ibid., p. xvii.
6. Ibid.
7. Ibid p.xviii.
8. Ibid pp. xix-xx.
9. Ibid p. xv.
10. Shlain, *Sex, Time and Power*, p. 95.
11. Other outer planets have only recently been discovered and so are not generally understood by astrologers as yet. From an astronomical point of view, Pluto has been reclassified as a "dwarf planet," not on equal footing with the other eight planets. There is no astrological evidence that Pluto does not work as an astrological influence. Some astrologers don't like to use the outer planets at all, but modern astrology includes them all.
12. Although people close to each other in age will share the influence of these planets, each person has a unique way of experiencing it. Astrologically we see this in the house placement and the configuration any of these planets makes with other planetary influences in a person's chart.

13. A mid-life crisis occurs roughly between the mid-thirties and the mid-forties and is accompanied by a series of astrological significators along the human continuum.
14. A trine or 120° aspect.
15. *Prometheus the Awakener* Spring Publications 1995
16. Sylvia Boorstein, *Don't Just Do Something, Sit There: A Mindfulness Retreat* (San Francisco: Harper, 1996).
17. A beautiful piece on this theme can be found in Tarnas, *Cosmos and Psyche,* p. 39: "Two Suitors: A Parable."
18. Liz Greene and Juliet Sharman-Burke, *The Mythic Journey: The Meaning of Myth as a Guide for Life* (New York: Fireside, 2000), p. 157.
19. For a description and discussion of a theory of the cultural container in which we live as dominator rather than patriarchal, read Riane Eisler, *The Chalice and the Blade: Our History, Our Future* (San Francisco: Harper, 1987).
20. Tarnas, *Cosmos and Psyche,* p. 99.
21. Alfred, Lord Tennyson, "In Memorium A.H.H." (1850). This quote comes from canto LVI: "Who trusted God was love indeed / And love Creation's final law / Tho' Nature, red in tooth and claw / With ravine, shriek'd against his creed."

Chapter 3: Holy Sparks

1. Helen M. Luke, *The Way of Woman: Awakening the Perennial Feminine* (New York: Doubleday, 1995), pp. 184-85.
2. Rabbi David A. Cooper, *God Is a Verb* (New York: Riverhead, 1997), pp. 1-3.
3. Judith Herman, MD, *Trauma and Recovery* (New York: Basic Books; Perseus Books Group 1992, 1997) p. 190.
4. See also *The Fourth Turning: An American Prophecy* by William Strauss and Neil Howe (New York: Broadway, 1997), an interesting book on the generations and their place in the culture.
5. The term "unraveling" is taken from *The Fourth Turning.* (See selected resources.)

6. Helen M. Luke, *Old Age* (New York: Parabola, 1987), p. 104. Furthermore she says, "Deeply ingrained in the infantile psyche is the conscious or unconscious assumption that the cure for depression is to replace it with pleasant, happy feelings, whereas the only valid cure for any kind of depression lies in the acceptance of real suffering. To climb out of it any other way is simply a palliative, laying the foundations for the next depression. Nothing whatever has happened to the soul. The roots of all our neuroses lie here, in the conflict between the longing for growth and freedom and our incapacity or refusal to pay the price in suffering of the kind which challenges the supremacy of the ego's demands. . . . The ego will endure the worst agonies of neurotic misery rather than one moment of consent to the death of even a small part of its demand or its sense of importance."
7. *Zen Mind, Beginner's Mind: Informal Talks on Zen Meditation and Practice* by Shunryu Suzuki (Tokyo: Weatherhill, 1970), p. 21.

Chapter 4: The Heart's Desire

1. For a more thorough discussion of this story, see Joseph Campbell, *Transformations of Myth Through Time*, Chapter 13: "In Search of the Holy Grail: The Parzival Legend" (New York: Harper, 1990).
2. William Butler Yeats, "The Second Coming," 1920.
3. Astrology as it is typically practiced in the Western world is considered to be tropical and geocentric. Geocentric means we put the earth at the center. Tropical means we determine the signs based on the seasons rather than the constellations. Therefore the first day of Aries is the day when the night and the day are of equal length and the days will get longer from that point until the first day of Cancer, when the days are as long as they get and will begin to get shorter. If we use the actual constellations to determine the signs we find a drift. For example, the first day of the constellation Aries rising with the Sun would fall in modern times during early March. This is due to the Precession of the Equinoxes, which, however fascinating, is not a topic we need to understand to become elders in times of chaos. For further reading, see *Hamlet's Mill: An Essay Investigating the Origins of*

Human Knowledge and Its Transmission Through Myth by Giorgio De Santillana and Hertha Von Dechend (Boston: Godine, 1992).

4. Matthew Fox, *The Hidden Spirituality of Men: Ten Metaphors to Awaken the Sacred Masculine* (Novato, California: New World Library, 2008), p. 16.
5. *The Cultural Creatives: How 50 Million People Are Changing the World* by Paul H. Ray and Sherry Ruth Anderson (New York: Harmony, 2000).
6. Robertson Davies, *Fifth Business* (Toronto: Penguin Canada, 1970).
7. Mark Helprin, *A Winter's Tale* (New York: Harcourt, Brace Jovanovich, 1983).

Chapter 5: Body and Soul

1. The relationship between the Sun and the Moon also includes the Earth. When the Moon is new, the Sun and the Moon are on the same side of the Earth; when the Moon is full, the Sun is on one side and the Moon is on the opposite side. A very interesting thing to note is that the Sun is 400 times larger than the Moon and it is also 400 times farther from the Earth than the Moon. From the perspective of Earth this creates the illusion that they are the same size. During a solar eclipse it is this factor that allows the Moon to blot out the Sun's light.
2. Sheila Ostrander and Lynn Schroeder, *Astrological Birth Control* (Englewood Cliffs, NJ: Prentice-Hall, 1972). The authors cite the work of Dr. Eugen Jonas, who discovered a very real correlation between a woman's fertility and the phase of the Moon a woman was born under. It seems that fertility increases every month when the moon returns to its original phase.
3. A number of reliable websites post the phase of the Moon on any given date. See, for example: http://tycho.usno.navy.mil/vphase.html
4. Alice Miller, *Drama of the Gifted Child: The Search for the True Self* (New York: Perseus 1981).
5. Derek Walcott, "Love After Love" in *Sea Grapes* (New York: Farrar, Strauss & Giroux, 1976).

6. Jonah Lehrer, "Grape Expectations: What wine can tell us about the nature of reality," *New York Times*, February 24, 2008. "The subjects consistently reported that the more expensive wines tasted better, even when they were actually identical to cheaper wines."
7. John O'Donohue, *Beauty: The Invisible Embrace* (New York: HarperCollins, 2004), pp. 3-5.
8. This version of "Beauty and the Beast" is taken from the website: http://www.paleothea.com/Gallery/PsycheAbductionBouguereau.html
9. Apuleius, *The Golden Ass: A New Translation*, trans. E.J. Kenney (New York: Penguin, 1998), pp. 72-73.
10. Ibid., pp. 71-110.
11. Helen Humphreys, *Wild Dogs* (Toronto: HarperCollins Canada, 2004), p. 86.
12. Luke, *Old Age*, p. 61.
13. Vedic astrology is the traditional Hindu branch of astrology.

Chapter 6: Responsibility

1. The first of the outer planets to be discovered was Uranus in 1781. (In Chapter 1 we discussed these transpersonal plants in relation to the early fifties.)
2. Jack Kornfield, *The Wise Heart: A Guide to the Universal Teachings of Buddhist Psychology* (New York: Bantam, 2008), p. 83.
3. The Saturn cycle of twenty-nine years can be roughly divided by four, which means that approximately every seven years there is a Saturn event. The first Saturn event is when we lose our baby teeth and begin to get adult ones around the age of seven. The second minor Saturn event is at age fourteen. At this time either we are brought into the fold of the larger community and expected to begin to take on some adult responsibility or we are not, in which case we challenge the status quo or drop out altogether. In contemporary western society we identify this period as adolescence and expect a certain amount of rebellion. In ancient time, when people had shorter life spans and society had more rigid limits, this was a time to begin adult life in earnest.

4. Natalie Angier, *Women: An Intimate Geography* (New York: Anchor, 1999), Chapter 13. You can also read about this in Leonard Shlain's book, *Sex, Time and Power,* Chapter 8.
5. Jean Piaget suggested that human evolution follows the schedule of a single human being. Think of the life cycle of *Homo sapiens* as analogous to the life span of an individual. See Shlain, *Sex, Time and Power*, pp. 270-271: "If seven years is to 110,000 years, as eighty (the average life span of an individual) is to *x* (the expected life span of our species), then, according to a whimsical exercise, our species would last to the ripe old age of 1.2 million years before going extinct (barring some self-imposed catastrophe). In this exercise, the current state of civilization suggests it has attained the equivalent maturation of a ten-year-old. Observing the daily events in the newspaper or on television, one might well concur with this assessment. Our species, unfortunately, does behave much like a ten-year-old. Not mature, but beginning to show signs of it. Gaining control over some human instincts but still relatively unsocialized. And he has become just strong enough to become dangerous to himself and others." Personally I think this is more descriptive of a 14 year old but I am fascinated by the overall concept.
6. Robert Bly, *The Sibling Society* (New York: Addison-Wesley, 1996), p. 237.
7. Bob Dylan, "Love Minus Zero/No Limit," *Bringing It All Back Home,* 1965.
8. This technique is called secondary progressions.
9. Luke, *Old Age*, p.107.

Chapter 7: Threshold: Chaos, Crisis, Change

1. Bernadette Brady, *Astrology: A Place in Chaos* (Bournemouth, UK: Wessex Astrologer, 2006).
2. Zalman Schachter-Shalomi., *Age-ing and Sage-ing: A Profound New Vision of Growing Older* (New York: Warner Books, 1995), p. 6.
3. Rumi, *The Essential Rumi*, translated by Coleman Barks with John Moyne (New York: Harper, 1996), p. 132.

4. Marion Woodman, interviewed by Sarida Brown, "Waking Up on the Threshold of Chaos," *Caduceus* magazine 60. www.caduceus.info/articles/woodman.htm.
5. Terry Pratchett, *Once More with Footnotes* (Framingham, MA: NESFA Press, 2004), p. 105.
6. http://www.stephenlewisfoundation.org/grandmothers.htm
7. See Barbara Marx Hubbard's website or read *Science and the Akashic Field: An Integral Theory of Everything* by Ervin Laszlo (Rochester, VT: Inner Traditions, 2004).
8. Luke, *Old Age*, pp. 45-46.
9. *Crones Don't Whine: Concentrated Wisdom for Juicy Women* by Jean Shinoda Bolen (San Francisco: Conari Press, 2003)

Chapter 8: The Path Less Traveled

1. If you would like to make a ritual of your own, I recommend *The Spiral Dance: A Rebirth of the Ancient Religion of the Goddess* by Starhawk (San Francisco: Harper, 1979).
2. We don't think of Lilith much anymore, but legend has it that she was banished by God for refusing to lie down beneath Adam. It was said she lived by the Red Sea and gave birth to demons. She was thought to be a presence in the night; arousing men sexually and stealing babies. See *The Book of Lilith* by Barbara Black Koltuv (Newburyport, MA: Nicolas Hays, 1986). If you would like a more astrological perspective on Lilith, see *Living Lilith: Four Dimensions of the Cosmic Feminine* by M. Kelley Hunter (Bournemouth, England: The Wessex Astrologer, 2009)
3. For more information on the goddess Hecate and her connection to elders, see *The Fabric of the Future: Women Visionaries of Today Illuminate the Path to Tomorrow,* edited by M.J. Ryan and Patrice Wynne (Berkeley, California: Conari Press, 1998), p. 163-68, and *Crossing to Avalon: A Woman's Midlife Pilgrimage* by Jean Shinoda Bolen (New York: HarperCollins, 1994), p. 272.

Selected Resources

Apuleius. *The Golden Ass: A New Translation.* E.J. Kenney, trans. New York: Penguin, 1998.

Angier, Natalie. *Women: An Intimate Geography.* New York: Anchor, 1999.

Banzhaf, Hajo, and Anna Haebler. *Keywords for Astrology.* Newburyport, MA: Weiser, 1996.

Bolen, Jean Shinoda. *Crossing to Avalon: A Woman's Midlife Pilgrimage.* New York: HarperCollins, 1994.

—. *Crones Don't Whine: Concentrated Wisdom for Juicy Women.* San Francisco: Conari Press, 2003.

Boorstein, Sylvia. *Don't Just Do Something, Sit There: A Mindfulness Retreat.* San Francisco: Harper, 1996.

Bly, Robert. *The Sibling Society.* New York: Addison-Wesley, 1996.

—. *My Sentence Was a Thousand Years of Joy: Poems.* New York: HarperCollins, 2005.

Brady, Bernadette. *Astrology: A Place in Chaos.* Bournemouth, UK: Wessex Astrologer, 2006.

Campbell, Joseph. *The Hero with a Thousand Faces.* New York: Pantheon, 1949.

—. *Transformations of Myth Through Time.* New York: Harper, 1990.

Cooper, Rabbi David A. *God Is a Verb.* New York: Riverhead, 1997.

Davies, Robertson. *Fifth Business.* Toronto: Penguin Canada, 1970.

Eisler, Riane. *The Chalice and the Blade: Our History, Our Future.* San Francisco: Harper, 1987.

Ellmann, Richard, and Charles Feidelson, eds. *The Modern Tradition: Backgrounds of Modern Literature.* Oxford: Oxford University Press, 1965.

Fox, Matthew. *The Hidden Spirituality of Men: Ten Metaphors to Awaken the Sacred Masculine.* Novato, California: New World Library, 2008.

Galland, China. *The Bond Between Women: A Journey to Fierce Compassion.* New York: Riverhead/Penguin, 1998.

Goldberg, Natalie. *Writing Down the Bones: Freeing the Writer Within.* New edition. Boston: Shambhala, 2005.

Greene, Liz, and Juliet Sharman-Burke. *The Mythic Journey: The Meaning of Myth as a Guide for Life.* New York: Fireside, 2000.

Helprin, Mark. *A Winter's Tale.* New York: Harcourt, Brace Jovanovich, 1983.

Hillman, James. *A Terrible Love of War.* New York: Penguin, 2004.

Humphreys, Helen. *Wild Dogs.* Toronto: HarperCollins Canada, 2004.

Hunter, M. Kelley. *Living Lilith: Four Dimensions of the Cosmic Feminine.* Bournemouth, England: The Wessex Astrologer, 2009.

Kornfield, Jack. *The Wise Heart: A Guide to the Universal Teachings of Buddhist Psychology.* New York: Bantam, 2008.

Koltuv, Barbara Black. *The Book of Lilith.* Newburyport, MA: Nicolas Hays, 1986.

Laszlo, Ervin. *Science and the Akashic Field: An Integral Theory of Everything.* Rochester, VT: Inner Traditions, 2004.

Lehrer, Jonah. "Grape Expectations: What wine can tell us about the nature of reality." *New York Times*, February 24, 2008.

Luke, Helen M. *Old Age: Journey into Simplicity.* New York: Parabola, 1987.

—. *The Way of Woman: Awakening the Perennial Feminine*. New York: Doubleday, 1995.

Miller, Alice. *Drama of the Gifted Child: The Search for the True Self.* New York: Perseus 1981.

O'Donohue, John. *Beauty: The Invisible Embrace.* New York: HarperCollins, 2004.

Ostrander, Sheila, and Lynn Schroeder. *Astrological Birth Control.* Englewood Cliffs, NJ: Prentice-Hall, 1972.

Pratchett, Terry. *Once More with Footnotes.* Framingham, MA: NESFA Press, 2004.

Ray, Paul H., and Sherry Ruth Anderson. *The Cultural Creatives: How 50 Million People Are Changing the World.* New York: Harmony, 2000.

Ryan, M.J. and Patrice Wynne, eds. *The Fabric of the Future: Women Visionaries of Today Illuminate the Path to Tomorrow.* Berkeley, California: Conari Press, 1998.

Rumi. *The Essential Rumi.* Coleman Barks with John Moyne, trans. New York: Harper, 1996.

Santillana, Giorgio De, and Hertha Von Dechend. *Hamlet's Mill: An Essay Investigating the Origins of Human Knowledge and Its Transmission Through Myth.* Boston: Godine, 1992.

Schachter-Shalomi, Zalman. *From Age-ing and Sage-ing: A Profound New Vision of Growing Older.* New York: Warner Books, 1995.

Shlain, Leonard. *Sex, Time and Power: How Women's Sexuality Shaped Human Evolution*. New York: Viking Penguin, 2003.

Smith, William. *Smaller Classical Dictionary*. New York: Dutton, 1958.

Starhawk. *The Spiral Dance: A Rebirth of the Ancient Religion of the Goddess.* San Francisco: Harper, 1979.

Strauss, William, and Neil Howe. *The Fourth Turning: An American Prophecy*. New York: Broadway, 1997.

Suzuki, Shunryu. *Zen Mind, Beginner's Mind: Informal Talks on Zen Meditation and Practice.* Tokyo: Weatherhill, 1970.

Tarnas, Richard. *Cosmos and Psyche: Intimations of a New World View.* New York: Viking Penguin, 2006.

Walcott, Derek. "Love After Love." *Sea Grapes*. New York: Farrar, Strauss & Giroux, 1976.

Woodman, Marion, interviewed by Sarida Brown, "Waking Up on the Threshold of Chaos," *Caduceus* magazine 60.

ACKNOWLEDGMENTS

Although it may be true that we are born and die alone, it is also true that everything we make in between is some kind of collaboration. Nowhere is this as clear as when it comes to raising a family or writing books. Like every author I have many people to thank and could easily write another chapter with the story of how they contributed to supporting me through this process. But I will endeavour to make a long story short.

I am grateful to and appreciate the love and support from the following:

All the elders in the groups I have taught; especially the first group who let me practice on them. The great thing about teaching is that in the end those who come to learn always end up teaching me at least as much as I teach them.

My good friends who have given me much needed emotional, as well as practical support and advice: Anne-Marie MacDonell , Carolyn Winter, Doug Williams, Jill Brant, Laura Phillips, Marie Frye, Orietta Minatel, Pat Hacker and Madeleine Byrnes. To each of you I am grateful for your intelligent support and wise counsel as well as for being my fellow intimate travellers on the journey from adult to elder.

My sisters Gloria Schwartz and Jane Kendall. There is nothing like a sister when you need someone to remind you who you are and are not.

My daughter Aurora Simmons. There is nothing like a child to teach you all the things you didn't learn when you were growing up.

Barry Pinsky for a location in which to write a first draft.

Meg Taylor for the intense and rigorous job of editing. Writing an astrology book that is not primarily for astrologers has its own challenges and I am truly grateful for the experience of working with such a skilled editor. A good editor is a bit like an angel: protective, wise in the ways of communication and compassionate; a messenger from the other world reminding you that people can't always read your mind, and then offering a path through an idea that opens it up to greater understanding.

June Bradley for her command of the comma.

Michael Barwick for inspiration for the single word definitions for the signs

Bonnie Campbell for holding my hand through the intensely challenging threshold of my own elder journey.

Helen Humphreys, Amanda Hale and Marni Jackson for taking the time to read and comment on this book.

Donald Raiche at Apple Farm Community for permission to use the quotes from Helen Luke's work.

Helen Humphreys for permission to use her poem from *Wild Dogs*.

As always I am thankful to astrology itself and all those who have been my teachers and guides along the way.

I would also like to thank the powers of synchronicity such as they are for three major offerings which kept me on the path of this project: The original inspiration which came in a moment, the owl which appeared at my feet just as I began the process of actually writing and the unusual and rare connection with Meg, my editor, at exactly the moment I knew I needed one.

I am glad I live in a world that is all relatives.